A NEW HEAVEN

A New Heaven

by

RICHARD HOLLOWAY

WILLIAM B. EERDMANS PUBLISHING COMPANY
GRAND RAPIDS, MICHIGAN

First published in 1978 by A. R. Mowbray & Co., Ltd., Oxford.

First American edition published in 1979
through special arrangement with Mowbray
by Wm. B. Eerdmans Publishing Co.,
Grand Rapids, Michigan 49503.

CONTENTS

PART 1

Prologue   7
1. The Day that Changed the World   13
2. Approach to the Day   18
3. Whose Christ?   26
4. The Christ of God   32
5. The Day   42
6. The Day After   48
7. The Third Day   54

PART 2

8. Longing   65
9. Responding   74
10. Praying   84
11. Blessing   101
12. Breaking   108
13. Transcending   116
Epilogue   121

ACKNOWLEDGEMENTS

Since this is meant to be a 'popular' paperback I have not cluttered the text up with footnotes, though I have quoted from other books. I would like, therefore, to acknowledge my use of other writers and to thank the following publishers for giving me permission to quote from them:

Faber and Faber for permission to quote from *Murder In The Cathedral*, by T. S. Eliot, *Collected Poems*, by Edwin Muir, and *The Unfinished Animal*, by Theodore Roszak;
Constable and Co. Ltd for permission to quote from *Peter Abelard*, by Helen Waddell;
J. M. Dent and Sons Ltd for permission to quote from *Letters To A Niece*, by Baron von Hügel;
Gill and Macmillan Ltd for permission to use the prayer *The Underground*, from Michel Quoist's *Prayers Of Life*;
Chapman and Hall for permission to quote from *Brideshead Revisited*, by Evelyn Waugh;
Chatto and Windus for permission to quote from *Autobiography*, by Edwin Muir. I would also like to thank William Purcell for his help in editing, and Richard Mulkern for forcing the pace and providing the title. A special debt of gratitude is owed to my wife, Jeannie, for taking time out from a very busy life to correct the proofs. Finally, I would like to acknowledge my gratitude to the people of Old St Paul's Church, Edinburgh for all their love and support over the years. Nothing in this book will be new to them!

Old St Paul's,   RICHARD HOLLOWAY
Edinburgh.

November 1978

PROLOGUE

'He laid down Abelard's close-written sheet on his knee, and his eye travelled to the window. The sun was still low in the east: why, wondered Gilles, should this level light transfigure the earth, beyond any magic of sunrise or sunset? There is more colour, he thought, in November than there is in August ... Perhaps, thought Gilles, it was because he himself was in his November, and the last day of it too, he added with a crooked smile, that the autumn seemed to him richer than any spring, and this pale persistent sunlight had a kind of heroic tenderness. There is no memory in spring, he thought, not even the memory of other springs: but a November day of faint sunlight and emerald moss remembers all things, the wild promise of the January days, snow-broth in February, violets in March, new-mown hay in June, dew-wet mint trodden underfoot in August nights, the harvest moon in September, the hunter's moon in October. Prudentius, he thought, was the November of the poets: Prudentius remembering

> How many times the rose
> Returned after the snows.'

I wonder if, in your contemplation of life, you have ever fallen into the mood of musing and affectionate regret expressed in this passage by Helen Waddell? I feel it often but, then, I was born in November and have always felt that a gentle melancholy was one of life's subtler pleasures. Even so, it seems to me that this November mood captures something profoundly true about our existence. It is particularly sensitive to the unremitting successiveness of nature and the passing of time. How brief are our summers! How swift are their joys! And how impossible it is to hold back the rush of time, to trap the fugitive moment and hold it. We cannot. We are all borne headlong into the unavoidable yet unrealizable future.

This mourning for lost time is really a mourning for ourselves. We mourn for ourselves, faced by death and surrounded by its symbols. It is the endless endingness of things which afflict us; all that coming to an end; all that going down into the grave; that inexorable tramp towards oblivion.

Everything is always coming to an end, as though life itself were only a rehearsal for that final exit. Just think of that last walk together over the hill on the last day of a green summer. Or think of that last supper on the night before departure, haunted strangely by the knowledge of its own finality. Think of all those doors closing and handkerchiefs waving, and that never endurable, yet always enduring clutch in the throat. Oh, and think how few are the Octobers in one life!

We must go even further, because the circle of the year and the certainty of our death, is but a miniaturisation of the devouring momentum of history and its tragedies. Like everything else, history is written on water, but we want it to congeal into permanence. Particularly do we want all the moments that transfigure time to continue, to stay their onward rush. It is Time, then, that we wish to be redeemed from; but all our schemes for self-redemption are themselves caught on the wheel of time. They cannot save us or impart the meaning of the whole. If time and life *have* meaning, the knowledge of the meaning can only be given to us from beyond time. The knowledge of the meaning can only come to us 'by revelation', which is mediated through sign and symbol. For Christians, the meaning of it all comes supremely in that strange, broken image of the young Christ, setting his face towards Jerusalem, to die there. Before he died, Christ left us bread for our journey through time. Of course, the meaning of these claims cannot be known in or contained by argument. Christians can only proclaim what they have experienced; what they have come to know in occasional frail stabs of recognition. That strange, tattered glory, the Christian Church, claims that there is a redemption from the rat-trap of time and successiveness and tragedy. It claims that there is a meaning which enfolds it, but it can only be spoken in riddles and parables and whispered poetry of bread that lives and endures for ever. It says that none of what we mourn for is lost: every rose from every summer that ever was, as well as the heart-break of every autumn, is contained in the glorious eternity of the Father who calls us to himself. He has given us living bread for the journey, food that time cannot wither. He bids us eat, else the journey will be too great for us. The bread he gives us (and we can only know this with our hearts) is the very flesh, the very life of his Son, who died for us, yet journeys with us still. For there is another image we live by. It does not replace the first one, the broken body of the young Christ; it adds another dimension to it. We look through the fitful stereoscope of Faith and we see that endless going up to Jerusalem, and that suffering and that dying. Then there is that hush before dawn in the garden where they laid him. No movement. Only the strange and wistful twilight in which we always see yesterday's grave. And then a sudden and terrible glory rises from that ancient sorrow, and suffering itself is transfigured, and time is transcended. The vision may fade and drift out of focus, but that is why we bear with gladness the primordial sorrow of the world.

'This is a riddle', you say. But how else does truth come to us, how else is our condition illuminated, broken open, but by riddles and signs and things that blow on the wind? 'Everything is in parables', said Jesus: strange, broken glimpses of a joy and a meaning and a final return when it will all be knit together. This book is about Jesus, the riddle God has set us. It tries to break open the meaning of his dying. It tries to show that it was for us he was broken. But it is also written in the conviction that he is risen and is still with us as we travel through time. It tries to show that he is still being broken for us. Still he goes with us. Still he feeds us as we make our journey. The first part of the book, therefore, meditates on the death he once died: he *was* broken for us. The second part of the book meditates on the life we can live in him *now*: he is broken for us still. Yesterday or today, it matters not: Christ is broken for you.

PART 1

God so loved the world that he gave his only Son, that whoever believes in him should not perish but have eternal life.
God sent the Son into the world, not to condemn the world, but that the world might be saved through him. John 3.16 and 17.

1. THE DAY THAT CHANGED THE WORLD

Ours is an age of what the psychologists call 'instant gratification': heat in our homes at the press of a button, light at the turn of a switch, and entertainment instantly available at a finger's touch. 'Instant coffee' is, perhaps, the most inclusive symbol of all: no need for all that lengthy grinding of beans and stewing of coffee grains; it's all there for us in an instant, a teaspoon away. (The Americans, apparently, are working on a special spoon that will instantly cool instant coffee, so that we won't even have to wait before consuming it!) Instant gratification. The same writ runs in almost every department of life, even in the acquisition of knowledge: it is all there for us, carefully tabulated and stored, ready for instant access. One of the institutions of our day is the prepacked knowledge parcel, the distilled essence of thousands of years of history, immediately available without the dusty duty of wading through yards of textbooks—instant history.

Any day now, some enterprising publisher will produce a series called, *All the Days that Changed the World*. It will provide us with easy access to all the pivotal events in our history, all the days that changed the world: what came immediately before and what followed after. Our century has been rich in these pivotal events. A volume on the twentieth century in this series would almost certainly begin with June 28th, 1914 in Sarajevo, and the shots that echoed round the world when the Archduke Francis Ferdinand and his wife were assassinated by a Bosnian nationalist. Those shots set going all the complicated horrors of the Great War, a war that certainly changed the face of history and tore up the map of Europe. The consequences of those fateful shots are still being worked out.

October 26th, 1917 was another fateful day. That was the day that the Petrograd Soviet, under Trotsky's leadership, set up a revolutionary committee which took over authority in the Province of Petrograd and finally set going the great and fateful drama of the Russian Revolution. You may have doubts about the continuing consequences of that muddled assassination in Sarajevo; you can have none about the present effects of those pivotal events in Russia sixty years ago. Those were certainly days that changed the face of history.

Let's jump to November 22nd, 1963. If you are over thirty you'll certainly remember that day and probably what you were doing at the time. That was the day John Kennedy was assassinated in Dallas. At the time it was an event of almost apocalyptic anxiety, though it probably had little effect on the main course of history. Who knows, Kennedy might have kept America out of Vietnam, and the turbulent sixties might not have been quite so turbulent for America, but one cannot be certain. Nevertheless, the assassination of President Kennedy was a pivotal event for many people, and it revealed the dark side of American society, as well as its nobility. 'Where were you the day that Kennedy died?' is still a question that many people are able to answer.

That day happened, all right, but there were one or two days, apparently, that nearly happened. A fascinating film was made some years ago about a plot to assassinate President de Gaulle, and even the fact that we all know it did not come off did not stop people asking, 'What might history have been like *had* it succeeded?' Novelists and historians have produced dozens of books on these events, providing minute by minute analysis of the events that led up to them and followed them. One thinks, for instance, of William Manchester's, *Death of a President*, and its plotting backwards and forwards of the circumstances and consequences of that poignant death in November 1963. A recent example of the passion for instant documentation, is the industry that grew up round the Israeli raid on Entebbe to secure the release of Jewish prisoners, hi-jacked by Arab terrorists. Books came out almost immediately, detailing that epic rescue, and a spate of films has followed. Days that changed the world.

Some of the events we have looked at could, arguably, be said to have changed all our lives in some sense, by radically changing the world we live in. But it is just as arguable that their effect varies from country to country and person to person. Obviously, the Russian Revolution has, in a very real way, affected all our lives because of its impact on the twentieth century, but it has clearly had most effect upon those closest to it: either those who have been oppressed by it, such as Solzhenitsyn and those like. him; or those who have used it to further their own will to power, such as Stalin; or the ordinary people of Russia whose day-to-day lives have been profoundly affected in all sorts of ways. Most historic events are like that: like a bomb explosion, their effect is most obvious and immediate at the point of impact, and it radiates outwards in diminishing degrees of intensity to the perimeter, where the only effect may be the noise of a dull explosion and the awareness that something is going on back there at the centre. We could say, then, that significant historic events operate *prospectively*, they influence and effect the future, but that their effectiveness is never absolute in its impact. Rather, the impact of historical events operates in widening waves of diminishing intensity, the way a pebble dropped in a pool radiates outward in ever wider but shallower ripples.

If we can take it that this more or less describes the effect of historic events, we can understand the scandal and amusement which Christianity arouses because of its claims for the significance of the events surrounding the death of Jesus Christ in Jerusalem, two thousand years ago. Christians hold that *his* death changed all time, and changed all time with the same impact. They believe that the death of that one man altered the status of *all* men. In the Gospel of John, for example, these words come from the mouth of Jesus and they make a universal claim for the significance of his own death:

'Now sentence is being passed on this world; now the prince of this world is to be overthrown. And when I am lifted up from the earth, I shall draw all men to myself.' 12.31ff. (Jerusalem).

The early Christian writers use various metaphors to try to capture something of the meaning of these events. The First Letter of Timothy, for instance, uses the image of slavery. Humankind was enslaved, but Christ's death has bought our release, ransomed us. The author says:

Jesus Christ gave himself as a ransom for us all—an act of redemption which happened once, but which stands for all time as a witness to what he is. 2.6 (Phillips).

Writing to the Romans, Paul describes us as enemies of God whom Christ has reconciled, and in the letter to the Ephesians he widens this claim to describe a peace which has been won between man and man, as well as between God and man. He writes:

'You had nothing to look forward to and no God to whom you could turn. But now, through the blood of Christ, you who were once outside the pale are with us inside the circle of God's love and purpose. For Christ is our living peace. He has made a unity of conflicting elements of Jew and Gentile by breaking down the barrier which lay between us. By his sacrifice ... he made one new man, thus producing peace. For he reconciled us to God by the sacrifice of his body on the cross, and by this act made utterly irrelevant the antagonism between us. Then he came and told both you who were far from God and us who were near that the war was over. And it is through him that both of us now can approach the Father in the one Spirit.'   2.12ff.   (Phillips).

All this is scandalous enough, but there is more to come! The death of Christ, the claim continues, is of cosmic significance: it affects the very destiny of the created, material universe. What we think of as sub-human and inanimate creation is affected by Christ's death; every atom in the universe is, by some strange chemistry, fundamentally altered:

'As he is the Beginning, he was first to be born from the dead, so that he should be first in every way; because God wanted all perfection to be found in him and all things to be reconciled through him and for him, everything in heaven and everything on earth, when he made peace by his death on the cross.'   Colossians 1.18ff.   (Jerusalem).

And the absurdity thickens because, the claim goes, the effect of this death upon history and the cosmos is not just *prospective*; it is not just concerned with what happened *after* Good Friday in the year 33. The Christian faith makes the apparently meaningless claim that this event is *retrospective* in its impact; that all who came before Christ are somehow implicated in its impact and that for them, too, something has changed. So the death of Jesus Christ has fundamentally altered the meaning and integrity of history itself, has rearranged the very destiny and progress of time.

I want to give some time to an investigation of this stupendous and, to many, outrageous claim. But there is no point in my attempting to adopt an attitude of critical detachment from the events in order to produce an objective and dispassionate account of the facts and their significance. This is impossible for two reasons. First of all, I have already taken up a particular attitude towards these events, the attitude we call faith. The faith I have in Christ and what he achieved is obviously not something I can lay aside for purposes of historical research. Whether I am aware of it or not, it will colour my attitude towards the history, as will your presuppositions and conscious or unconscious assumptions. It is not possible to purge my mind in this way, and it is honest to confess one's interest. But, on the other hand, as a Christian I am very interested in getting as close as I can to the strict *facts* of the case. Truth is important to me. Simone Weil said that anyone who put Christ before truth had already rejected Christ, because he is the Truth. So it will not be possible to suppress the facts, or doctor them. They must stand as they are. But that, anyway, is not much of a problem. The basic facts are hardly in dispute—it is their significance which is debatable. And here we must obviously move from the surface of history to its inner meaning, from time to the meaning of time. Boris Pasternak wrote some mysterious yet highly significant words: 'Everything that happens in the world takes place not only on the earth that buries the dead, but also in some other dimension which some call the Kingdom of God.' He meant that there was an inner core to the reality of life which gives it meaning, even when it seems most horrifyingly devoid of meaning. There is a double drama at work; or rather, there is one drama, but its real meaning is not yet completely disclosed and has to be sought for beneath the superficial flux of events. The same profound duality, or two-dimensionality is captured in some words which T. S. Eliot put into the mouth of Becket in his great play, *Murder in the Cathedral*, though they can certainly be applied to Christ:

'It is not in time that my death shall be known;
It is out of time that my decision is taken ...
If you call that decision to which my whole being gives
entire consent.'

I want, now, to look at the events of Christ's passion and try to understand them historically. The full impact of the claim that is made is something which will, finally, call for that attitude we call Faith or Trust or Commitment, that response from within, that answer which comes from our whole being to a challenge, an invitation which is made, quite personally, to each one of us.

2. APPROACH TO THE DAY

One of the most difficult human gifts to acquire is the gift of historical imagination. For some people it is almost impossible to divest themselves of their own presuppositions and prejudices and submerge themselves imaginatively in another period of history. Most of us judge the past by the present and we limit our understanding of the past by so doing. One of our common assumptions today is that religion and politics ought, to a large extent, to be kept separate: religion belongs to the private sphere and must be kept there, while politics concerns man in his public relations and national and international encounters. But that is really a very modern view of the matter. Until comparatively recently, most of mankind had a unitary view of society in which no clear separation was made between religion and politics. The Jews probably had the most consistent view of this matter. Their ideal society was a theocracy in which every aspect of life was governed and controlled by the nation's contract or covenant with God. In the days of Jesus the Jews were a subject people, a colony of Rome, but their thinking and their expectations were certainly governed by this unitary view of reality, and no clear cut division between the religious and the political can be made when we think about their history.

Nevertheless, there was, in our Lord's day, a division between the two, but it was a division which was bitterly contested and which was never absolute. Broadly speaking, we could say that the Romans were largely in control of civil and political matters, while the religious estabishment, the Temple hierarchy, was left in charge of the religious life of the nation. That was the theory and largely the practice, but it kept breaking down, because the Jews were a race who were dominated, one might say obsessed, with the idea of the Total Society, purged of all false and impure elements, reigning as God's elect people over a new heaven and a new earth. It was the conflict between this consuming and eruptive vision and the Roman political strategy which led, in the year 70, to the final destruction of Jerusalem and the ejection of the Jewish race from their homeland. So our Lord lived and died in a land which was a bubbling cauldron of religious and political tension, and he managed to align both religious and political forces against himself. I want to discuss the reasons for his death, therefore, under two separate headings: the religious, and the political; not because there was an absolute distinction between them (at the end, as we shall see, they were hand in glove together), but only because it is a convenient distinction to make for closer examination.

Why was Jesus crucified? Because he was a threat to the whole structure and tradition of the Jewish religion. I want now to unfold and justify that answer.

There are several noble religious systems in the world. A religion is the way man organizes his search for God and his response to God. Some of man's most amazing discoveries and some of his most poignant heroisms have been made in the name of religion. And the Jewish religion is probably the most sublime and complete religion of them all. In essence it involved a high way of perfection through the observance of a law which was acutely and exhaustively detailed in its application: it covered every aspect of living and cast a religious mantle upon all things. It was not law as we think of it: law as prohibition, law as the necessary boundary and limitation placed against our selfishness; law as that organized restraint which is an essential part of all communal relations. The Law to the Jew was much more than that. It was a whole way of life, and it was just as concerned with positive observance as with negative avoidance. Kept perfectly, it might unite a man with God.

'Ah, how happy those of blameless life
who walk in the Law of the Lord!
How happy those who respect his decrees,
and seek him with their whole heart,
and doing no evil,
walk in his ways!
You yourself have made your precepts known,
to be faithfully kept.
Oh, may my behaviour be constant,
in keeping your statutes.
If I concentrate on your every commandment,
I can never be put to shame.

I think from an upright heart,
schooled in your rules of righteousness.
I mean to observe your statutes;
never abandon me.' Psalm 119.1-8 (Jerusalem).

There has never been a nobler or more complete religion than the Jewish one, yet its very sublimity and nobility was its greatest weakness. It was, for one thing, extremely elitist. The proper observance of this minutely detailed tradition was something which the common man found impossible, and to the Gentile who was outside the Law, it was, in many of its requirements, incomprehensible. It thus seemed to place a vast and complicated minefield between man and God, which man must cross with extreme care if he would make his way to God. This mine-field consisted of hundreds of commandments and ordinances which covered everything, from circumcision and the cleaning of vessels and the ritual washing of hands, to exclusive prohibitions against whole classes of technically unclean people. While it exalted some, others it reduced to despair. What could you do if you were, say, a tax collecter, following a trade which was itself beyond the spiritual pale, unclean, impermissible? Or if you were a prostitute? Or a half-caste? To these spiritual proletarians, the Jewish Law was a way, not to God, but to despair and hopelessness and a sense that they were without God in the world. The staggering and scandalous and ultimately suicidal thing which Jesus did was to place God himself outside the Law alongside those who were outcasts and sinners. In some mysterious words of Paul, Jesus, in order to save those who were under the Law's curse, those who were beyond its perfecting power, became himself a curse, the ultimate lawbreaker. And Jesus performed this extraordinary act of demolition not only in words but in actions: he neutralized and relativized the absolute status of the Law, and drove its guardians into a murderous and protective rage. I want to look at several ways in which he did this.

Human beings have a wonderful built-in genius for turning means into ends, for taking some entirely practical activity which is done for the sake of something else and turning it into something which is done for its own sake. And it is very far from being an entirely bad thing. On the contrary, many of the things we value most in life are of this sort. We do them simply because we enjoy doing them, because they add richness and colour to life. Trooping the Colour is a good example. Originally a regimental standard, or colour, was paraded round the soldiers just before a battle. Trooping the colour was a serious and practical matter, which served to help soldiers recognize it, when the need arose, in the confusion of battle. Those days have long past, but we still do it. The difference is that nowadays we do it because we enjoy doing it. It has become something we do for its own sake. It adds a tone and texture to life, which would be very dull without such things. In a sense the British monarchy is another example, although here there are quite a few practical advantages as well. One of the main uses of the monarchy is to supply a means of expressing our need for colour and pageantry and to provide a focus for our self-awareness as a nation. Of course, there are always lots of people who are against all these things. They are usually persons of a dour and puritan disposition, natural commissars, who think that life ought to be stripped of all these unnecessary flourishes and reduced to strict geometrical logic. There are always plenty of them in ecclesiastical circles. They would like our worship to be stripped of all its delicious inessentials and be reduced to a dull earnestness. They've got their way with many of the new liturgies, but they'll never win entirely because, as I said, we have a need for this sort of thing. If we are deprived of it in one way, we'll find alternatives, but we'll have it one way or another, because mankind does not live by the bread of necessity alone. We need all the unnecessary things if we are to be fully human: we need poetry and music and roses and custom and ceremony, and all the sheer and wonderful nonsense of simply being alive. God protect us from all the commissars in our midst who would deprive us of our baubles! W. B. Yeats captures what I'm trying to say in the last stanza of his poem, *A Prayer for My Daughter*:

'... and may her bridegroom bring her to a house
Where all's accustomed, ceremonious;
For arrogance and hatred are the wares
Peddled in the thoroughfares.
How but in custom and in ceremony
Are innocence and beauty born?
Ceremony's a name for the rich horn,
And custom for the spreading laurel tree.'

But, as in all things human, there is a dark and terrible side to this amiable tendency. We could say of the examples I have given so far, that we have taken certain customs and institutions which once had a purely practical use, and we now use them to serve a purely human need: we do them now because we like them because, in a mysterious way, they give us pleasure. There is also a tendency which is clean contrary to this one. It will take some custom, some purely practical affair which was introduced to benefit humanity, to make life more convenient or less stressful, and it turns it inside-out, so that it is now kept for its own sake, long after it has ceased to serve humanity. This is what had happened to the Jewish Sabbath. For the Jews (as for many Christians after them) the Sabbath became an absolute which existed in its own right. Its sacred character was hedged about and protected by a whole range of defensive fortifications which prohibited travel and work and medical care. What had happened to the Sabbath is a very common reversal in man's religious systems. A tradition or custom is developed which was originally meant to assist man's life, but it ends by becoming a burden upon him. It was meant in the first place to be what philosophers call 'an instrumental good', something that is good *for* something else, such as mankind's welfare, and it ends by becoming what they call 'an intrinsic good', something which is good in itself and must be observed for its own sake. This happened to the Sabbath. It was a wise tradition, designed to protect man the worker from his own folly or from the exploitation of his employers. It was meant to be good *for* man. It ended by being a burden *upon* man. Jesus reversed all this with the simple statement: 'The Sabbath was made for man and not man for the Sabbath', and by that saying, and by his own actions on the Sabbath day, he took an axe to everything in the world that exploits and dehumanizes man in the name of an abstract principle. How widely that simple revolutionary claim can be applied: 'The State was made for man and not man for the State', would be an appropriate and timely version. Jesus healed on the Sabbath. He took his disciples for a picnic on the Sabbath. In short, he *humanized* the Sabbath, turned it to the service of man and not to his enslavement. And it was noted down and held against him by the religious establishment of his day.

That was only the beginning. One of the strongest and most reliable elements in the tradition about Jesus was that he ate and drank with sinners, with those who were outlawed, those who were held to be outside the scope of God's concern. This was a motley company which included Gentile soldiers, tax-collectors (quislings and collaborators with an enemy power), prostitutes, drunkards and sinners in general. He also had a free and open relationship with women in a society where their rights were severely circumscribed. And he supported this scandalous freedom in table-fellowship with a whole series of explosive parables all designed to make the same point: to remove the massive but common assumption that men and women had, somehow, to qualify for God's interest, God's love. He asserted the revolutionary doctrine that God loves sinners while they are yet sinners; that he cares for the unrighteous and the unclean; that his mercy hovers over all, infinitely caring. By his actions and his parables he detonated that mine-field which had been carefully assembled by the religious genius of centuries: he simply blew up one of man's noblest creations because, he said, it had come between God and his love for his children and nothing could come between it and them. God loves his enemies! God loves those who don't believe in him! His love is a perfect and ineffaceable radiance which is not turned on by our supposed goodness nor turned off by our alleged wickedness. It was a message which reversed all the great spiritual systems of self-development and discipline by which men and women have sought to save themselves. He came telling us that they could not save us, but that he would. Unless you grasp this you have failed to understand the central scandal of the Christian faith: Christ saves us from religion ond law; we are no longer justified by them, saved by them, but only by his grace. And the wonderful thing about all this is that it is the enormous security which God gives us by his unswerving love which provides the only sound basis for real holiness: no longer a neurotic, moralistic craving for a sterilised perfection; now a relaxed and unselfconscious following of God's will in joy. And this affects our belief, too. We no longer have to screw up our minds like the Queen in Alice in Wonderland to believe six impossible things before breakfast, because we are not justified by the work of our faith! Faith, like holiness, grows out of the experience of being justified and accepted. Faith grows from the experience of the love of God. It is true that in the Christian Church we have tamed and trivialized and sentimentalized that unbelievable claim of Christ's, but even in the Christian Church, which is but old Judaism in new guise, these claims still escape and release us.

And this is possibly the right place to correct a possible wrong impression. I am not setting up the Christian Church over against the Jewish religion as a more perfect religious system. It isn't. The Christian Church witnesses to Christ, points to him, but it does not contain him and, alas, it has frequently reversed his teaching and returned to that which he came to destroy. It is a sad truth that Christianity has itself become a great religion of law, binding men and women with regulations and red tape. It did not take the Church very long before it started reversing the teaching of Christ. And we do it still. We bind men and women hand and foot because, like the contemporaries of Christ, we fear that terrible freedom he brought, we resile away from the insane mercy of God. We would rather make another religious system out of it that we can manipulate. No, the Church does not possess this Christ, indeed, it has often been his enemy, as I have often been his enemy but, thank God, we are not saved by the Church, but by Christ who still dies to save his enemies.

Why was Christ crucified? Because he subverted human religion. No religious system controlled or limited or directed man's access to God. No human group, be it Judaism or Christianity has control of the road to God, or has the right to erect innumerable tolls along that road and collect fees from those passing through. Christ came to bring us instant and universal access to God. There is no human institution which guards the way to God, there is no palace guard which controls the traffic around the heavenly throne. No group has a monopoly of the Divine Favour. It is available for all and comes to *them*. It sees us while we are a great way off, while we are still imperfect, unacceptable and impure, smeared and bleared with guilt and shame, soiled with constant unfaithfulness, and it comes to us and embraces us without regard to our condition. Those who had made a business or a way of life out of controlling the passes to God's favour could not possibly look upon this teaching with anything but murderous disapproval, since it threatened the very grounds of their existence. They had long since acquired the rights in this particular commodity and like all powerful and privileged groups who ever were, they organized themselves against threats and challenges to their monopoly. In the Gospels we see their resentment against Jesus growing and stirring and rising like a flood until it overwhelms him. And the main point of their accusation was just, though they did not realize it. What Jesus did and said implied, whether or not it explicitly claimed, that he was of God and from God and knew God in a way that no

other man ever did nor could. He claimed to know the very
nature of God in a way that only an insider could know it. So
they accused him of claiming to be the son of God. 'We have
a law and according to that law he ought to die, because he
has claimed to be the Son of God'. The irony of that statement
is that men cannot allow God to be God, to be himself as he
is, without *their* control and consent. *That* God they will always kill. As we shall see, the killing of God is a permanent
human activity.

3. WHOSE CHRIST?

The Christian Church has received very mixed reviews in history. Very often the name-calling is a family affair, with opposing groups of Christians denouncing one another as anti-Christ or worse. There is, for instance, a man from Glasgow who goes all over the world and appears at ecumenical services holding a placard which says, in effect, that everyone is out of step with Jesus except himself. By now, he is almost an essential part of any great ecumenical occasion, and he is certainly the part which the press pays most attention to. But this is not a modern phenomenon. Twenty years after his death, and possibly before that, those who called themselves Christ's followers had started the well-known game of defining those who were in and those who were out. It has continued ever since and it is not an edifying story. Anyone who knows his history will not find the witness of the Church to Christ a universally compelling thing. It is always a mixture of the sordid and the sublime. St Augustine used the picture of Jacob wrestling with the angel to explain this paradox:

> 'Look at this man, on one side he was "touched" by the angel with whom he wrestled, and that side shrank and was dried up; but on the other side he was blessed. It is the same man, one part of him shrunk and limping, and the other blessed and strong ... The shrunken part of Jacob signifies the evil Christians, for in the same Jacob there is both blessing and limp. The Church of today still limps. One foot treads firmly, but the other drags. Look at the pagans, my brothers. From time to time they meet good Christians who serve God. When they do, they are filled with admiration, they are attracted, and they believe. At other times, they see evil-living Christians, and they say, "There, that is what Christians are like." But these evil living Christians belong to the top of Jacob's thigh, which shrank after the angel had touched it. The Lord's touch is the hand of the Lord, straightening and giving life. And that is why one side of Jacob is blessed, and the other shrunken.'

But it is not only Christians who play this game. It is an

intriguing fact that most people want to claim Christ for their side. And those who are outside the Church play this game with as much zest as the contentious and disputatious Christians. Communists frequently claim Christ as their's, and some of them do it in a very self-righteous way, claiming that they and only they have really been faithful to Christ's message. At the other extreme, the late Lord Beaverbrook wrote a book in which he firmly placed Christ on the side of modern capitalism and its philosophy of private enterprise. Almost any group seems to be able to see in Jesus some confirmation of their own point of view. The wonder is that they feel it necessary to enlist his support. This extraordinary man still dominates our thinking and attitudes in all sorts of ways, and while people scarcely concern themselves with the Church's blessing, it does seem important to them to have the blessing of Christ.

Each age seeks for this seal of approval according to its own preoccupations. I remember in the 1960s during the days of the Campaign for Nuclear Disarmament, a Canadian TV producer made a film which was a modern life of Jesus, and he showed him as a ban-the-bomb protester who was eventually murdered by the military-industrial establishment because of the threat he posed to their interests. This has been followed by other portrayals of Christ, some diametrically opposed to the picture of him as an angry radical, such as the lyrical and romantic hippy Christ of *Godspell*.

Each generation seems to need to portray Christ as a contemporary, the embodiment of the chic or dominant culture-hero of the day. One of the most persistent themes is that of Christ as the political revolutionary, the utopian dreamer, who gave his life to bring in a better world and whose followers must do the same. This is a very contemporary picture of Christ and there are several political theologies going round at the moment which cast him in this role. The Black movement in the *USA* claimed Christ for their exclusive cause, for instance: Christ was black and the freedom he preached was, quite specifically, the liberation of the black from white oppression. This *was* the Gospel for the black man, and it could be understood in no other way. An even more contemporary variant on the same theme is emerging from Latin America today, where Christ is seen to call the millions of oppressed in that vast and troubled continent to shake off the tyrannous yoke of the powerful elites who govern them so cruelly. Christ is a revolutionary and his Gospel calls his followers to the way of resistance to all dictatorship. Both of these modern accounts of the significance of Christ state specifically that the Gospel must closely involve itself with the overthrow of capitalist regimes and their replacement by socialist societies. The theme of Christ as the first socialist is a very old one in Christian thinking. According to this interpretation of Christ, the answer to the question, 'Why was Christ crucified?', is quite straightforward: His death was a state execution. It was an absolutely predictable response by the political establishment to one who came proclaiming its overthrow and who called the wretched of the earth to rise up and challenge their oppressors. There is no doubt that this interpretation of Christ has been and still is extremely potent. It is a constant theme in the history of mankind's attempt to create the just society.

Now, there can be little doubt that, whatever the real motive was, Christ seems to have been executed on a charge of insurrection and political conspiracy. The accusation which was written out and pinned above his head on the cross said that he claimed to the 'King of the Jews', a claim which was certainly political if interpreted in the obvious way. From what we can gather of his trial and appearances before Pilate, it was claimed that he spoke against Caesar; and he was executed by Pilate, however cynically, as having been charged by the loyal leaders of the Jerusalem Religious Establishment with sedition. How seriously can we take this picture of Christ?

Again, we must try to use our historical imagination. The Palestine of the time of Jesus was politically volcanic and religiously volatile, and one gets the impression that it would take little to set the fuse that would blow the whole thing up. We know that this happened, finally, about forty years after our Lord's death, when the Romans, their patience finally exhausted, brutally destroyed the Jewish homeland of Palestine and set going two thousand years of wandering by God's ancient people, the Jews. At the top were the Roman administrators who were, as a rule, happy to leave the local rulers to manage affairs, provided taxes were paid and the peace kept. It was a system that worked well for many colonies, but the mix in Palestine was too explosive. The ecclesiastical establishment, and the Herods, the client kings of the Roman power, had a strong interest in maintaining the status quo. Change could not possibly be in their interest; it never is for the privileged, who have learned to live with and work the System. It is a lesson which the Christian Church learned very quickly, when it had attained power and responsibility and a strong investment in political stability. There is scarcely an epoch when the Church has not been happy to lend its support to any regime, however evil, provided its own institutional security is not threatened. So let us not judge the rulers and high priests of the Jewish nation too harshly. They are our representatives.

Below that level there was a seething market place of political and religious movements, some escapist, some activist, dedicated to the violent overthrow of the Roman occupation. We hear echoes of these movements in the New Testament, and they must have provided a complicated background to the ministry of Jesus. There seemed to be a few Zealots, a group committed to violent revolution, among his followers, and some believe that Judas Iscariot belonged to a particularly enraged sect of this sprawling movement, the Sicarii, the dagger-men, who went in for select political assassination. Christ must have aroused the interest and expectation of many of these groups. He was, to begin with, a wandering teacher, travelling light, whose very life-style was in marked contrast to the established forces in Church and State. He preached a message of hope to the poor and was ironically dismissive of riches, and he *had* something, what we'd now call *charisma*, leadership quality to an ultimate degree and an ability to use language itself as a weapon which turned against the complacent and powerful who anxiously protected their own privileges. What a gift such a man would be to the revolutionaries who then, as now, were almost infinitely sub-divided into groups of competing intensity and ideological purity! Doctrinal extremists, whether political or religious, are always prone to this sort of distintegration, which is why opposing power groups find them easy to deal with. They use up most of their energy fighting each other, unless a sufficiently compelling leader arises who welds them into a single group—the mark of all great revolutionary leaders. Was that the task of Jesus? Was that why they executed him?

There is no doubt that the political anxieties of the day contributed to his death, but it is impossible to cast him as a first century Che Guevara. We need not go to his trial to find our evidence. The trial accounts in the New Testament do not give us enough to go on, and some hold, anyway, that the accounts there do not square with what is known of legal procedure in those days (though then, as now, courts could be 'rigged'). No, we must go back to what we know of his life and sayings, because it is there that we find the real refutation of the claim that Christ was simply a political revolutionary.

In the first place, then, there was no *strategic hate* in Jesus. The successful revolutionary must inculcate a level or potency of class or group hatred in his followers if he is to succeed in overthrowing the tyrant he opposes. The enemy must be objectified in a way that dehumanizes him, in order to make it easier to liquidate him when the time comes. There is none of this in Jesus. On the contrary, he *reverses* the process of group hatred, by preaching love of the enemy and non-resistance towards those who would exploit us. Surely the very opposite of the revolutionary ideology and its rhetoric and glorification of violence! It is for this reason that those who developed 'the Strong Man' theory of human destiny, such as Nietzsche, have dismissed Jesus as an emotional weakling who unmans his followers.

Secondly, there was no exclusive *group loyalty* in Jesus. The most compelling thing about him was his freedom. His freedom enabled him to make bitingly accurate assessments of all human pretensions, but he never suggested that these weaknesses were group or structural characteristics. And he moved freely among every type of person: Roman soliders, tax-collectors, the rabble of the city, and the rich and powerful from both the civil and religious establishments.

Thirdly, he did not, as all revolutionaries do, preach *a conspiracy theory* to explain human evil and suffering. The fault did not lie in the socio-economic structure, but in the heart of man whence came all evil and its consequences. He went to the real root of our human dilemma: our nature and its taint of sin and alienation from God.

Finally, he did not produce the stock revolutionary answers to the stock questions. They tried to trap him with the question which sorted out a man's politics: whether or not it was right to pay taxes to Caesar. He neatly avoided the one-way street they tried to drive him up by affirming that Caesar had a legitimacy, but that it was far from ultimate.

But the real answer to the revolutionary accusation is that Jesus was not against any man or group, but for them all. He wept over Jerusalem, he did not plan to blow it up, and his anger at his opponents was the tragic side of his love for them, since they were so blind to their own real needs. It is impossible to pin Jesus down and claim him exclusively for any single section of humanity. The Jews, we read, once came to try to make him a king, and he passed through their midst and went his way. And this is so of any group or sectional interest which would capture him and domesticate him for their own cause. He is unclassifiable, except as the supremely free man. It was this freedom which he preached: freedom from everything except the glorious bondage of the service of God, in which alone lay perfect freedom. He made everything on this earth relative and provisional, unable to bear any ultimate loyalty: only God must have that. All else will fail, and the placing of ultimate loyalty upon purely temporal goals and ends is the most tragic and stultifying of all idolatries. Christ will not be contained by us, nor enrolled or recruited into our pet sectional interests. He belongs to us all, but not on our terms, only on his own. God is not the possession of any group however dedicated and self-sacrificing they are. Christ passes through the midst and makes his own way whenever we try to enrol for Right or Left or Centre.

What could be more unpopular than that? Where *did* he stand, this Will o' the Wisp, who would not genuflect to anyone's pet theory? Soon all the myopic and self-interested enthusiasm for him turned to hatred as he constantly passed through their midst, as he rejected all the chains of office they tried to thrust upon him. Who was he, to march to the beat of a different drummer from everyone else? Just who did he think he was? Soon, those revolutionary hosannas turned into 'crucify, crucify', and yet again Jesus went his own way.

It is ironic to note that they released a noted revolutionary, a paid-up Party member called Barabbas, on the crowd's demand. But Jesus? Jesus they delivered up to be crucified.

4. THE CHRIST OF GOD

One of the most irritating things about Christians is the way they seem to keep changing their ground. One moment they will be in agreement with you concerning the particular details of a certain event, but the next moment they have moved away from history to some other dimension, some place out of time which, they claim, is yet contained within or comes bursting through the event you have just agreed about. You can be talking about the same thing, and suddenly it is not the same thing at all. There is something of this wilful and infuriating ambiguity in that famous saying of Blake's:

' "What," it will be questioned, "when the sun rises, do you not see a round disk of fire somewhat like a Guinea?" O No, No, I see an innumerable company of the heavenly host crying, Holy, Holy is the Lord God Almighty.' Christians always seem to be operating on two levels at once. To him they are not two levels, but to the non-Christian who does not see with the eyes of Faith, they most decidedly are. Christians do this with all sorts of things. They take bread and wine, for instance, and do something with it and it remains bread and wine and yet, they say, it is no longer just bread and wine; it is charged with a whole new weight of meaning and significance. In other words, Christians seem to be permanently bi-focal, seeing certain events with a depth and a background which recedes into eternity.

I have already quoted the words of Pasternak which capture this mysterious duality: 'Everything that happens in the world takes place not only on the earth that buries the dead, but also in some other dimension which some call the Kingdom of God.' The main focus of this double-meaning for the Christian is the crucifixion of Jesus. So far I have investigated that event on the level of history. The account I have given may, to some, be controversial, but it is an arguable conclusion from the facts that we have. I have tried to account for the wave of opposition and hostility to Jesus which finally engulfed him in blood. I have dealt with publicly observable events, with history. And on that level the story, of course, is over. Yet another compelling and attractive figure has been done to death by the System, and not by any means the last. Another moving defeat of the sort that are immortalized in folk music all over the world.

Yet it is just here that the Christian makes one of those spectacular changes of gear: he still acknowledges the defeat and the death and the dereliction; he still acknowledges the human agents who planned and plotted this event to their carefully orchestrated conclusion. He agrees with all that, but at the same time and of precisely the same events he starts using words which seem to describe a completely different event: for defeat and dereliction, he reads victory and glorification; instead of seeing confident men confidently plotting, he sees the same men as actors in a drama not of their own devising, so that this event is not theirs at all. Shortly after the conclusion of these events, when all his followers forsook him in a headlong flight from danger, we find the same men proclaiming that this event was God's, yes, God's doing. In the words of the Acts of the Apostles: 'This man who was put into your power by the deliberate intention and foreknowledge of God, you took and had crucified by men outside the Law.' And even earlier than this, Paul is telling us: 'Jesus was put to death for our sins.' 'God did not spare his own Son, but gave him to benefit us all.'

So this event which we call the crucifixion of Christ was the action and direct intention of God. In it, according to the Christian faith, God acted decisively on behalf of mankind. It was not one of those apparently senseless killings that disfigure our history. This killing was different, because God was involved in it from the very beginning. It was no accident. And here we are back to that strange double-focus which Christians see in history. T. S. Eliot puts certain words into Becket's mouth in *Murder in the Cathedral* which capture this transcendent duality:

'A Christian martyrdom is never an accident, for Saints are not made by accident. Still less is a Christian martyrdom the effect of a man's will to become a Saint, as a man by willing and contriving may become a ruler of men. A martyrdom is always the design of God, for his love of men ... It is never the design of man; for the true martyr is he who has become the instrument of God.'

And this cannot be known except by that strange knowledge we call Faith; and there can be no arguing about or into faith.

The contemplation of this event which is more than event, speaks decisively to our hearts and we answer from within, we hear the word it addresses to us, we recognize what it means, and we make our response. Henceforth, it is no mere event in time: it is now an opening into the very meaning of time, a glimpse into the very heart of God. It is *God's* action we see there. As an old hymn puts it: 'Faith our outward sense befriending makes the inward vision clear.'

What, then, is the meaning of this event? What is the action of God in this event about? In answering that question, we can only grope about in the dazzling obscurity that surrounds the cross. Christians have known that God acted then, have felt the effects of it and do so still, but they have never found an entirely satisfactory set of words which adequately capture what this event is all about. As in all talk of the mystery of God's dealings with us, they have had to use metaphor and analogy, like their Lord who frequently began his teaching by saying 'The Kingdom of heaven is like ...' Before examining some of these analogies, however, I want to make an important distinction.

We are dealing here with a fact which is also a mystery. Let me give you an example: Creation. Creation is a fact: it exists. Something has clearly happened, and we are affected by it. So Creation is a fact, but it is also a mystery. How did it happen? What does it mean? Who did the creating? Creation is a mystery, and because it is a mystery we can never put a complete answer to any of these questions into words. We are always struggling to express the inexpressible, to utter the unutterable, to eff the ineffable, as someone put it. The work of Jesus Christ in saving the world and redeeming mankind is like creation: it is fact and mystery. It is fact: men and women know they have been changed by it. They know that something has happened to them and to the universe. They know that what Christ did has made a difference that rings on through time and eternity. It is a fact that many know and that many *long* to know: they want Christ to be *their* Saviour. Christ's work is a fact and a mystery, and men have striven to express that fact in word and music and art and lives lived and deaths died. They have struggled thus, to explain and translate the mystery. They have built up vast theories, grand designs of doctrine and speculation, all designed to explain and set forth that fact above all facts, that mystery, of all mysteries the most tremendous. We call that attempt Christian

Doctrine, though Thomas Aquinas, after dedicating his life to its perfection, called it straw. Doctrine is a heart-breakingly impossible attempt to contain and describe the uncontainable and the indescribable. The New Testament does not give us theories, does not give us a doctrine of salvation, though it has become the happy hunting ground of doctrinal speculators. What the New Testament does is to proclaim the fact, affirm the fact, trumpet and celebrate the fact; and there are always a handful of theologians in every generation who believe that that and that alone is what the Church should still do. Nevertheless, in proclaiming the fact of our salvation through Christ, the New Testament uses certain metaphors, certain communication devices, which do not contain the mystery, but which set going a reaction, a recognition, a penny-dropping process in the minds of the listeners. There is, for instance, the metaphor of struggle and conflict:

'Now sentence is being passed on this world;
now the prince of this world is to be overthrown.
And when I am lifted up from the earth,
I shall draw all men to myself.'   John 12.31.

The First Letter of Timothy uses the image of slavery: humankind was enslaved, but Christ's death has bought our release, ransomed us:

'Jesus Christ gave himself as a ransom for us all—an act of redemption which happened once, but which stands for all time as a witness to what he did.'   1 Tim. 2.6.

Writing to the Romans, Paul describes us as enemies of God whom Christ has reconciled, and in the letter to the Ephesians he widens that claim to describe a peace which has been won between man and man as well as between God and man. There are other metaphors, such as the great metaphor of Justification or Acquittal, a legal metaphor which proclaims that Christ won a verdict of innocence for all us guilty ones.

Men and women have come closest to capturing the nature of the salvation won in Christ, not in prose but in poetry. In particular, the hymnody of the Christian Church is a treasure trove, full of historical riches which show us how Christians of other ages have tried to express their understanding of the meaning of Christ. There have been three great models offered to explain our salvation, three great theories, though frequently their protagonists have treated them as infallible truth. We can learn something from each of them. Each emphasises an important facet of salvation doctrine. Fortunately, each of these great theories has been expressed in hymn and song. It is always worth while to ask ourselves how these expressions of the meaning of salvation resonate with us today, whether or not they retain anything that is relevant and appropriate.

The earliest theory, and the one we find in the most ancient hymns, is called The Classical Theory by theologians, classical because it is the most primitive, both in the way in which it is expressed, and also in the sense that it represents the earliest attempt at a theoretical explanation of the work of Christ. In essence it is this: it sees mankind as a land which has fallen into enemy hands. We belong to God, he is our rightful ruler and king, but his rule has been usurped by the great enemy of God, the Devil, the present Prince of this World. He has usurped God's rule, and holds us in bondage. He has colonized us and we live in bondage to his imperial rule. We are not free to serve God, free to be good, free to love, free to be our true selves, free not to die. Like the Israelites in Egypt, we are slaves, held fast in bitter bondage, bound under the heel and tyrannous jurisdiction of the devil. And Christ is the great liberator. He comes forth from God to do battle against the devil. Like a commando from the Almighty, he comes in disguise, as an undercover agent, to deceive and confuse the devil. He comes right into enemy territory and begins a campaign of sabotage. He quietly sows the seeds of rebellion against sin and selfishness and the reign of evil. He gathers round him a guerilla army who join him in his battle against the usurper, and whom he trains for the mopping-up operations that will follow his great battle. Then he moves towards the great and final encounter: he takes on Death itself, that great sign and seal of the dominion of the devil, the last enemy. He submits to that and destroys it from within. In hand to hand combat he breaks the very rule of death, shattering its grisly power over men. The final sign of that victory is the Resurrection: that is the great moment, the hoisting of the colours of God over his wounded creation; the previous blood prevails; the devil is routed and taken captive; captivity itself is held captive and death and sin and the shedding of eternal tears are forever stopped, because the strong son of God has prevailed. That was the great message of liberation preached by the early Church. You'll find it proclaimed with passionate intensity in hymn after hymn. A fifth century bishop put it all into words which we still sing and can scarcely better.

'Sing, my tongue, the glorious battle, Sing the ending of the fray;
Now above the Cross, the trophy, Sound the loud triumphant lay:
Tell how Christ, the world's redeemer,
As a victim won the day.'

We also find it in these familiar words from Charles Wesley:

'Love's redeeming work is done:
Fought the fight, the battle won:
Lo, our Sun's eclipse is o'er!
Lo, he sets in blood no more.'

The classical theory of the atonement has enduring appeal. Do not dismiss it too lightly. It is undergoing something of a renewal with the emergence of Liberation Theology in the Third World, which still sees salvation as a struggle against oppression, in a way that brings the classical theory right up to date.

The second great theory comes in several different forms, but it is usually called The Substitution or Satisfaction Theory. It is a theory which many find congenial, and it is particularly dear to the hearts of Evangelicals and our friends in the Salvation Army. It has enormous power, and has won many souls for Christ. This theory emphasizes man's personal sinfulness, rather than his captivity to the devil: it is private rather than corporate, concerned with individual souls, rather than with mankind as a whole. It sees his state not so much as the result of an invasion from Satan, but as an act of willed collaboration on his part. We have gone over to the enemy; we have sold ourselves into bondage because of our own sinfulness and wilfulness. The devil has paid the full market price for us and we cannot buy ourselves out of bondage, since we have sold ourselves utterly. We cannot redeem or ransom ourselves. We have no savings left, nothing that we have not pawned or mortgaged. But Christ acts as our substitute. He pays our ransom by giving himself. He swops himself for us, in the way that one or two people substituted themselves for parents in the Nazi death camps. Christ is our Substitute. Another variant of this theory, with less of a biblical basis, is the idea that God

himself demands satisfaction from us before we can be reconciled with him. Rather in the way a council tenant, having
been evicted for arrears, must first pay off his debt before he
can be offered another house. He must make satisfaction. But
how can we? We are bankrupt. *Christ* pays the price, he satisfies the justice of God. The hymn that expresses the theory
with least offensiveness is Mrs Alexander's famous hymn,
written in the nineteenth century:

'There is a green hill far away,   Without a city wall,
Where the dear Lord was crucified   Who died to save us all.

He died that we might be forgiven,   He died to make us
good;
That we might go at last to heaven,   Saved by his precious
blood.

There was no other good enough   To pay the price of sin;
He only could unlock the gate   Of heaven to let us in.

The great strength of this theory, sometimes called The Objective Theory, is that it takes human sinfulness seriously. Its
weakness is that it can be expressed in a way that drives a
strange wedge between God and Christ, whereas the witness
of the New Testament is that 'God was in Christ' and that
our salvation was won for us *by* God *through* his Son, and
not *from* God *by* his Son.

The third great theory is called The Exemplarist Theory,
though we might call it The Subjectivist Theory or The Psychological Theory, because it sees the work of Christ as
having its effect by changing people's attitudes as they think
about and contemplate the great and loving sacrifice of Christ.
As we study how he lived, we cannot but be moved by his
great love and seek to copy it in our own lives. But there is
more, even, than this. Our very understanding of God is
altered, because the life and death of Jesus show us what God
is like. He is our servant and our victim. He rescues us, ran-
soms us from the bondage of our anxious selfishness, not by
an act of power and overwhelming justice, but by an act of
self-emptying love. He *woos* us, this God of ours. He defeats
us by the lengths to which his love will go. Insecure people,
uncertain of their acceptance by other people, unsure that they
are loved, push and push others to the limit in their search for
re-assurance, until their friends or relatives can take no more
and can go no further. They are then confirmed in their origi-

nal sense of rejection: when the chips are really down, they think, they are not truly loved, there is always a limit.

But it is not so with God. He allows us to push him right out of life onto the cross. He spares not his own son, the very desire of his heart, his very heart itself. God was in Christ, not separate from him, but in him, working through him, going the other mile, offering the other cheek, giving the final assurance, taking the very last step, offering us the ultimate proof that we are his, that he really loves us and will never forsake us, no matter how furious and self-destructive *our* rejection of *him* is. He absorbs it all—all our hate and all our sorrow; he bears it in his own body on the tree; he takes it upon himself. The cross is the final example of God's love: it is the action which finally secures our release from our own fears and loneliness; the proof that God is still for us even though we are against him. The death of Christ in all its bleakness and beauty opens up for us the very heart of God, and what we see there is the unconquerable love which guides the universe, not with overwhelming power but with invincible weakness, and it moves *us* to heart-broken love. The great medieval theologian, Peter Abelard, will be for ever associated with this story. His re-discovery of it was bred of his own experience of torment and rejection. In her magnificent novel, *Peter Abelard*, Helen Waddell imaginatively reconstructs the occasion on which Abelard's mind begins to move towards this account of the cross of Christ.

'"My God," said Thibault, "what's that?"
From somewhere near them in the woods a cry had risen, a thin cry, of such intolerable anguish that Abelard turned dizzy on his feet, and caught at the wall.
"It's a child's voice", he said. "O God, are they at a child?"
"A rabbit", said Thibault. He listened. "There's nothing worrying it. It'll be in a trap. Hugh told me he was putting them down. Christ!"
The scream came yet again.
Abelard was beside him, and the two plunged down the bank.
"Down by the river", said Thibault. "I saw them playing, God help them, when I was coming home. You know the way they go demented with fun in the evenings. It will have been drumming with its hind paws to itself and brought down the trap".'

Abelard went on, hardly listening. "Oh God", he was muttering. "Let it die. Let it die quickly".

But the cry came yet again. On the right, this time. He plunged through a thicket of hornbeam.

"Watch out", said Thibault, thrusting past him. "The trap might take the hand off you".

The rabbit stopped shrieking when they stooped over it, either from exhaustion, or in some last extremity of fear. Thibault held the teeth of the trap apart, and Abelard gathered up the little creature in his hands. It lay for a moment breathing quickly, then in some blind recognition of the kindness that had met it at the last, the small head thrust and nestled against his arm, and died.

It was that last confiding thrust that broke Abelard's heart. He looked down at the little draggled body, his mouth shaking. "Thibault", he said, "do you think there is a God at all? Whatever has come to me, I earned it. But what did this one do?"

Thibault nodded. "I know", he said. "Only—I think God is in it too".

Abelard looked up sharply. "In it? Do you mean that it makes Him suffer, the way it does us?"

Again Thibault nodded. "Then why doesn't He stop it?"

"I don't know", said Thibault. "Unless—unless it's like the Prodigal Son. I suppose the father could have kept him at home against his will. But what would have been the use? All this", he stroked the limp body, "is because of us. But all the time God suffers. More than we do".

Abelard looked at him, perplexed. "Thibault, when did you think of all this?" Thibault's face stiffened. "It was that night", he said, his voice strangled. "The things we did to— to poor Guibert. He—"

Thibault stopped. "I could not sleep for nights and nights. And then I saw that God suffered too. And I thought I would like to be a priest".

"Thibault, do you mean Calvary?"

Thibault shook his head. "That was only a piece of it—the piece that we saw—in time. Like that". He pointed to a fallen tree beside them, sawn through the middle. "That dark ring there, it goes up and down the whole length of the tree. But you only see it where it is cut across. That is what Christ's life was; the bit of God that we saw. And we think God is like that, because Christ was like that, kind, and forgiving

sins and healing people. We think God is like that for ever,
because it happened once, with Christ. But not the pain. Not
the agony at the last. We think that stopped".
Abelard looked at him, the blunt nose and the wide mouth,
the honest troubled eyes. He could have knelt before him.
"Then, Thibault", he said slowly, "you think that all this",
he looked down at the little quiet body in his arms, "all the
pain of the world, was Christ's cross?"
"God's cross", said Thibault. "And it goes on".
"The Patripassian heresy", muttered Abelard mechanically.
"But, oh God, if it were true. Thibault, it must be. At least,
there is something at the back of it that is true. And if we
could find it—it would bring back the whole world".'

This theory of the Atonement has always to the orthodox been
faintly tinged with heresy, but it has always had enormous
emotional power, and while it may contradict the rather static
ideas about God in traditional Theism, it does speak to the
heart. It is movingly expressed in Ireland's great hymn:

'My song is love unknown,
My saviour's love to me.
Love to the loveless shown
That they might lovely be.'

And we find the same theme in that other great and popular
hymn:

'When I survey the wondrous cross,
On which the Prince of glory died,
My richest gain I count but loss,
And pour contempt on all my pride.

Were the whole realm of nature mine,
That were a present far too small;
Love so amazing, so divine,
Demands my soul, my life, my all.'

So, the sublime and staggering claim which is made, is that
God was himself our victim, that he was acting in that horrify-
ing execution on our behalf. It is this view which seems to me
to have the greatest contemporary appeal. Without in any way
repudiating the truth or significance of the other two approaches, it is this approach which I wish to develop.

5. THE DAY

What difference did it make? Christians make large claims for the execution of Jesus Christ on that hill outside Jerusalem. They claim that it altered the meaning of all things, past and present and future. But what can that claim mean? It does not mean that all history is to be rewritten, and altered in the writing, in order to fit some new theory. There has been a lot of that way of altering history in our century, as tyrants have torn up the truth and put down their own version of events. It is not like that. The death of Christ does not, cannot alter the facts of history. All the misery and all the pain is still misery and pain. Those tears are still wet and that blood is real and those departures still break the heart. No, the past is not altered. It is forever fixed in its grandeur and horror. The frieze on the vase does not move. The past is not altered. Nor is the future. Calvary made little or no difference to the story of the way of the world. It made no decisive difference. He died at three in the afternoon. This decisive event, this event of cosmic significance, was accomplished by the afternoon tea-break. If we had the statistics of the Jerusalem Police Department we'd see that during the hours that followed the death of Jesus, until the beginning of the Sabbath, there were four murders, three rapes, several fights in taverns in the city and one major fire; seventeen people died of natural causes, including five children. No, nothing was altered, nor ever has been. You are not altered. Nor am I. My heart is still divided. My life is still disordered, running between the bitter and the sweet. Nothing is altered by this event. And yet, says the faith I try to hold onto, and yet everything is changed. A decisive event has occurred, not only in time, but in Eternity. It is not in time but out of time that this event is known, and it is an event which is revolutionary and total in its scope, its scale and its effect.

But let us now look at the event itself before we seek to interpret it. The earliest and starkest account of the crucifixion is found in Mark's Gospel. Already in the other accounts we see a subtle process of translation and interpretation taking place. The Gospels were all written long after the event was experienced, and looking back they see the event bathed in a radiance that it cannot have had at the time. It is almost impossible to place yourself on Calvary and purge your mind of what followed three days later, but we must try.

This was no glamorous execution of a confident and jaunty actor on the stage of history. History is full of stories of the elegant fortitude of men who have gone to their deaths with style. I think of Charles I, wearing two vests on the morning of his execution so that he would not shiver with the cold on the scaffold and allow the spectators to think he was afraid. And I love the humour of Thomas More as he clambered up the rickety steps to the scaffold and addressed these words to his guard: 'I pray you, Master Lieutenant, see me safe up, and for my coming down let me shift for myself.' Before he knelt for execution he made a brief speech, protesting that he died the King's good servant, but God's first. But the story I love best concerns the execution of Montrose. When a Puritan railed at him for combing his hair on the scaffold in readiness for his execution, Montrose said: 'While my head is my own I dress and arrange it. Tomorrow when it is yours you may treat it as you please.' Christ did not die with such elegance. Make no mistake about it, he died alone, forsaken by man and by God. Roman crucifixion was not a quick or painless death, like beheading or hanging, where the anguish is all in the anticipation. Crucifixion was both torture and execution, execution by torture, slow death by impalement.

When they came to arrest Jesus it was the middle of the night. We know he had not slept. We know he was in an agony of uncertainty and apprehension. Can it be that when they finally came for him he was filled with a sense of relief? In one of his novels Solzhenitsyn describes just such a feeling invading a Russian intellectual when he is finally arrested during one of Stalin's purges. All uncertainty now banished, he goes off with the KGB with a high head and a strange lightness in his step. Certainly, Jesus faced his captors with diginity and assurance. In the hours that followed he was dragged through six trials. He was taken before Annas, the father-in-law of Caiaphas the High Priest; then he was taken before Caiaphas himself; then he was taken before a hastily summoned meeting of the Sanhedrin, the High Court of the Jews; next there was the first trial before Pilate, who sent him to Herod; and finally, he was brought back to Pilate for final sentence. The detail as we have it may not be totally accurate, but there was no doubt at all that he was put through a most gruelling night. During these hours he was beaten up at least twice, probably with that impersonal professionalism which is the trademark of the secret policeman the world over. During the trials he was bound, his arms pulled back tightly and roped painfully to his body. Immediately after Pilate had passed the sentence of death, he sent him away to be scourged. Scourged! The word for us has a cosy, almost domestic ring about it, suggesting little more than an energetic application of a little Vim to a dirty pot. But there were few more painful ordeals than Roman scourging. The victim was stripped, and he was either tied to a pillar in a bent position with his back exposed so that he could not move, or he was stretched rigid upon a frame. The scourge was made of leather thongs studded with sharpened pellets of lead and pieces of bone. It literally ripped a man's back to pieces, so that many lost consciousness under the lash and many emerged from the experience raving mad. After more sadistic horseplay by the soldiers, they led him away to be crucified.

The procession to the place of execution always followed the same pattern. The criminal was placed in the centre of a hollow square of four Roman soldiers; in front there walked a herald carrying a board on which the charge was painted. It was later pinned above the head of the victim. The criminal was taken to the place of execution by the longest possible way, through the busiest streets and through as many of them as possible, so that he might be a dreadful warning to others. As he went, he was lashed and goaded. He was forced to carry at least part of his cross. When they reached the place of execution the cross was assembled. The upright beam was usually in place in its socket and the victim was forced to carry the cross beam. At this point it was customary to give the victim a drink of medicated wine mingled with gall, to help drug him for the pain that was to follow. Jesus refused the drink. Half-way up the upright beam of the cross there was a projecting ledge of wood, called the saddle, on which part of the criminal's body rested, or the weight of his body would have torn the nails clean through his hands. At that moment the victims cursed and swore and shrieked and spat at their executioners. We are told by Luke that Jesus prayed: 'Father forgive them, for they do not know what they are doing.' Usually only the hands were nailed, the feet being loosely bound to the upright beam of the cross. The criminal

was stripped naked. But the real terror was yet to come. The
real terror of crucifixion was that it was a lingering death. A
man might hang on a cross for days, tortured by flies, parched
with thirst, burned by the sun by day, and frozen by frost
during the night. Most victims of crucifixion died raving mad
after days of unendurable agony. If a man refused to die or
begged to be put out of his misery, it was the custom, after a
day or two, to pound him to death with the blows of a mallet.

But the greatest torture of all was the prolonged and unconsolable loneliness as death and the final darkness crept
down. Mark gives us only one word from the cross, and that
the most terrible: 'My God, my God, why hast thou forsaken
me?' Jesus died forsaken. The God he called Abba, Father,
whose love and care he celebrated in unforgettable language,
was nowhere near him as pictures and images swam through a
mist of pain and anguish. Mark tells us that he hung there for
six hours, from nine in the morning till three in the afternoon,
through the hottest time of the day. He died at three in the
afternoon, utterly deserted. Mark tells us that a few women
watched from a distance, but all his closest followers had
deserted him. They had all melted away. Death is, at its final
moment, something we must all undergo utterly alone, but
most of us will want some human comfort to encourage us for
the last journey. Christ died alone. He went down into the
deepest well of rejection and loneliness. The cross is the sign
of absolute torment; physical, spiritual and emotional.

When we think about the cross, therefore, we are thinking
about one of the grimmest instruments of torture ever devised
by the cruel imagination of man. It is difficult to think of a
modern equivalent. Maybe being trapped alive in a burning
car would would be as painful, though scarcely as protracted
a death. How would twentieth century people react to a
religion which used as its symbol a screaming victim impri-
soned within a blazing car, and kept a day called DEATH ON THE
ROAD DAY? Or I suppose certain diseases are as grim as crucifixion. What about a religion that made a gaily painted brain
tumour its symbol, and kept a holy day in honour of carci-
noma? Preposterous, isn't it? Positively ghoulish, yet for
centuries the Christian Church has looked to the cross as its
symbol. Millions have kissed it, clung to it at death, sung
songs about it: 'When I survey the wondrous cross' ...
'Sweetest wood and sweetest iron, Sweetest weight is hung on
thee.' The cross has been part of the Christian way of life since

the earliest years. An early theologian says: 'At each journey and progress, at each coming in and going out, at the putting on of shoes, at the bath, at meals, at the kindling of lights, at bedtime, at sitting down, whatsoever occupation engages us, we mark the brow with the sign of the cross'.

As I think back over the years I have been preaching about the cross, I realize that I have almost always *moralized* it. I have urged people to deny themselves present gratification for the sake of long-term satisfactions. I shudder as I think how I have trivialized the cross, instrumentalized it, made it a symbol of our need for discipline, our need to deny ourselves. All that is true enough, but it is not what the cross means, not remotely what the cross of Christ means. The cross is not a dreadful warning to us. It is not a moral exhortation, scaring us into goodness. That would be nothing to sing love songs to. No, the cross is none of that. The cross is, simply and staggeringly, the sign and certain seal of God's unconquerable and unquenchable love for us. We may run from it, be too ashamed to face it. Our hands may cover our eyes that we have handled him so. His love abides. And it is we who have done this to him. Ours were the bitter words that goaded and taunted him. Ours was the anger that crimsoned his skin with his own blood. Ours were the hands that drove in the nails, that pierced the side. We were the ones who lifted high the cross and dropped it in its socket with shuddering and sickening finality. And we do it daily. We set him to a perpetual shame. The universe is alive with the unending noise of hammer-blows. With unwearying and unremitting anguish we try to kill his love for us. And we cannot. We cannot destroy that love. It wears us down with its mute and eloquent acceptance of all the self-hatred we pour upon him. If only we could really see it, the cross is God's answer to all those questions that torment us about our own evil and the evil and suffering of the world. It is God's answer to every anguished 'Why?' that we utter. 'Why if there is a God does he allow this to happen? Why does he let pain and misery stalk the universe?' Indeed, the cross is a fit emblem, the perfect sign of that protest, for here is a monstrous and cynical death with not a single redeeming feature; a death which is stark and jagged with evil. WHY?

Good Friday ought either to make us atheists or drive us to a scandalous and releasing insight into the very nature of God. The cross is either the last word of man, the final symbol of all the meaninglessness that stunts and crushes him, or it is the last word from God himself, speaking to us through our own anguish, comforting us through our own wounds. For the Church says that Christ, far from being forsaken by God, was God himself, descended into the utmost depth of the human experience, tasting torture, death and abandonment. God was *in* Christ, fully experiencing the utter Godlessness of his children. And how can words capture that insane and quivering paradox? God identifies with us, even in our very atheism! So when we say that something happened which changed things for all time between God and man, we do not mean that it changed God's attitude towards us, that he was bought off by the blood of Christ. We mean that God changed *our* attitude to *him* by placarding his love for us in the cross of Christ. The cross proclaims two great truths.

First, God loves us like that! He goes into the very extremity of our rejection to demonstrate the unconquerable nature of his love. Nothing that we do is sufficient to drive him away. He defeats us only by his love, that love that waits and abides eternally and watches over us in the torment of our rejection of everything that belongs to our peace.

Secondly, that, far from being an aloof and unconcerned observer of our anguish, who for divine sport has wound up his little universe and lets it run how it may, he is himself in it with us, endlessly trudging down all those roads that criss-cross history, rag on his feet, eyes dark with pain, endlessly moving up to Jerusalem to be put to death. History is full of strange stories of God Incognito, slipping in behind the barbed-wire, journeying through his creation on broken feet, the Way-faring God, the Suffering Christ, crucified till the end of time.

So, nothing is changed by this day, yet how can anything be the same once you have seen its meaning? At last we see it, the inner meaning, the pattern beneath the flux of chance, the shrapnel fragments of exploding time. And the face we see beneath it all is the ravaged and lovely face of the Christ who struggles on through all the world's Good Fridays, travelling on and on, always setting his face to go up to Jerusalem and die for us.

6. THE DAY AFTER

The day after a death is always the day of remembering, the day of regret. It is the day when everything is too late. For Peter it must have been a day of unbearable anguish as he remembered the last look Jesus gave him. St Luke tells us that after the arrest of Jesus they brought him to the High Priest's house. Peter followed at a distance and stood outside in the courtyard, watching. That courtyard was the scene of his three denials of Christ and of the moment when Jesus gave him that last look. We are told by Luke that 'the Lord turned and look at Peter ... and Peter went out and wept bitterly'. What a look that must have been! It would not have been one of our kind of looks: An 'I-told-you-so look'—'See, Peter, I said you'd deny me, didn't I?' That kind of look gets a familiar reaction: embarrassment, resentment, self-justification. But this look was different—I can hardly say the words, it was so different: 'And the Lord turned and looked at Peter.' I know that look well. It is a look dark with the pain of unconquerable love. Can you bear the thought of a love that is filled with pity for its own betrayer? Our Lord, as the lonely terror of his Passion mounts, turns and looks at Peter, but not with reproach. That would be easy to bear—reproach, mute accusation; we could bear that, but not this look of ravaged and awful love. How can we bear that? How can we stand to think of a love like that? Our Lord was filled with care and anxiety for Peter, because he knew how the pain of his betrayal would haunt and torture him, turning and turning inside him, making him sick with self-loathing; because there is no agony like the agony of a failure you can never undo. Jesus felt all this for Peter, knew Peter's self-inflicted suffering, and had pity on it. He turned and looked at him, his eyes dark and large and ravaged with longing. But now it is too late, and Peter remembers that look with an anguish that will not be still.

It was the same when they laid him on that rough wood. His thoughts were for his executioners. 'Are you hurt my child? Did the wielding of that heavy hammer upon my body bruise your hand? Father, forgive them, forgive my children, they

know not what they do. Do not lay this crime to their charge.'
Was ever love like that? No wonder we cannot tolerate it;
no wonder we crucify it—because we cannot bear it, it is too
much for us. We can only hammer at it with averted eyes—
or weep. 'The Lord turned and looked at Peter, and Peter went
out and wept bitterly'.

That ancient look haunts the whole of man's history, and
what breaks the heart is its finality. It always comes too late for
us. We catch it across a great gulf. It is always seen on the
other side of regret. 'Too late, too late have I loved thee.' It is
like a word just remembered when the train door has closed.
It is a sudden premonition at the bottom of the ward as we
turn to wave to that white face above the blankets. It is an
injury we did and cannot call back. It is a single rose laid upon
a coffin. It is that mute and swollen hurt that burns and burns
inside us for all the ways we never took, the love withheld, the
vision never followed till a better day might come. Then it
it is that we feel that look upon us, that ancient, stabbing
glance of pity for all our failures, for what our life might have
been and is not and won't be now, because it is too late, isn't it?
It is always too late. We miss happiness 'by seconds, at an
appointed place'. Just think of what we are and the glory we
have missed! A little more effort here, a deeper faithfulness
there, a tiny increase of endurance and moderation, and we
might have built our lives above regret. And now we feel the
numbing surge of discontent at what is and what might have
been. And Jesus grieves for us in our bitterness. 'The Lord
turned and looked at Peter ... and Peter went out and wept
bitterly.'

The bleak and awful fact is that there is no human answer
to this crushing sense of loss, this suffocating regret for things
not done that ought to have been done, or done that ought not
to have been done; or words spoken better left unsaid; and all
those words we never uttered or never wrote, and now it is
too late and we regret them all. If we think of it all, if we think,
like Peter, of that look, that look across the impassable gulf of
death, we would surely drown in our own sorrow. Too late!
Each of us knows that look, or one day we shall: that last and
single and tender look thrown like a cord we fail to catch across
the final separation. There would be no second chance, were
it not that it is God who looks at us there.

The cross and passion of Jesus Christ are not isolated events
in history. The death of Christ shows us God's way with us

for ever. He suffers at our hands. He does not overwhelm us with unavoidable power. He does not wield a rod upon us for our sin. Or present himself to us to shatter all our doubt. Instead, he goes among us gently, *on wounded feet*. He turns and *looks* upon us. And you must grasp this, if you would know God. So many people say: 'Why does God allow suffering? Why does he stand back and let it go on?', as if he were away somewhere, while we mourn. I have tried to say one thing, and one thing only in this book, because it is the very heart of the Christian good news and if men and women could only hear it, it would, in Abelard's words, 'bring back the whole world'. It is this: it is *God* who suffers, God whom we smite and destroy; it is God who crowds the road round the ruined city, travelling with ancient patience among his wounded children; it is God who is laid to rest in all those tiny graves; it is God who falls upon the barbed wire under the searchlight glare. God is the Victim, the Eternal Victim, and his only weapon is a look of suffering love. 'The Lord turned and looked at Peter ... and Peter went out and wept bitterly.'

Christians should weep for themselves, for their children and for the ravaged and tormented world he looks upon. He knows us and all our defeats and every day we do him to death. Augustine says:

'Christ is still journeying whither he has gone before. For Christ went before us in the head, and Christ follows in the body. Christ is still here toiling; here Christ suffered at Saul's hands ... Christ is still here in want; here Christ still journeys; Christ here is sick, Christ is here in bonds.'

It is obvious, is it not, that the death of Jesus has changed nothing. The creation still groans in travail, as Paul said. It is easy for some of us, perhaps, to ignore some of the agonies of creation for a little longer, wrapped round as we are with the transient comforts of a way of life which is even now destroying itself. We are like a group of squabbling and prosperous businessmen playing poker in a lounge on the Titanic as it approaches mid-Atlantic. We have, perhaps, forgotten what it is like to suffer, but soon we'll know, and the cold and the darkness will be colder and darker for our years of ease. Yes, it is easy for us to forget the men entombed in the Lubyanka or to ignore the little graves at Dimbazi. We do not see the swollen bellies and the dead eyes of Christ's little ones just over the Southern horizon. *We* have not lived with the sound of mortars, nor have we dragged our lives endlessly down dusty roads, always a little ahead of advancing troops. We have not known that, though most of the world has. But we have known suffering in our own way and according to our fashion. We, too, must all die, though discreetly and with reserve. And we know sickness and separation, in our way. There is despair here, even amidst the cushions and behind the cheerful curtains. Yes, in our way, we have known, continue to know suffering.

And what difference does Easter make? I know what that look of Jesus means. I know the suffering and the love and the defeat that is all love knows, but what is this Resurrection, why all this carolling about some joyful Eastertide? What difference does *that* make to all that tears and wrenches us apart? It makes *no* difference. It will not stop a single bomb or feed a single child. It will not bring back the dead we love or hold those in life we cannot bear to lose. It will not change that X ray plate or bring back an unfaithful lover. Christ is still crucified and that ancient look of ravaged love still pierces the universe. Like the Crucifixion itself, the Resurrection makes *no* difference. Still he stands in that cold and hostile courtyard and look at us. So weep. There is no drying of your tears.

And yet, it makes *all* the difference. The story of the look that pierced Peter was only told, only *could* be told, *after* the raising of Jesus. Peter told the story of his own betrayal after an event which changed everything yet changed nothing. Here the preacher is himself upon the cross, for where are the words that will capture this elusive and certain wonder? Peter, to the very end of his life, betrayed Jesus. Nothing changed in Peter, and yet everything changed, because he had seen something through his own tears which enabled him to go on through betrayal after betrayal, right up to the end. Peter discovered that there need be no permanent failure in his life because nothing he did was able to overcome the love of Christ. Every time he fell, Christ picked him up. The reconstitution of Peter was never a single event. It was a constant renewal of the love for Christ which fought with his own weakness. Shortly after the death of Christ, according to the twenty-first chapter of John's Gospel, Peter's threefold denial was overlaid by a threefold confession of love.

'When they had finished breakfast, Jesus said to Simon Peter, "Simon, son of John, do you love me more than these?" He said to him, "Yes, Lord; you know that I love you." He said to him, "Feed my lambs." A second time he said to him, "Simon, son of John do you love me?" He said to him, "Yes, Lord; you know that I love you." He said to him, "Tend my sheep." He said to him the third time, "Simon, son of John, do you love me?" Peter was grieved because he said to him the third time, "Do you love me?" And he said to him, "Lord you know everything; you know that I love you." Jesus said to him, "Feed my sheep. Truly, truly, I say to you, when you were young you girded yourself and walked where you would; but when you are old, you will stretch out your hands, and another will gird you and carry you where you do not wish to go." (This he said to show by what death he was to glorify God.) And after this he said to him, "Follow me." '

And Peter followed Christ—as well as he could. Almost as poignant as the scene in the courtyard on the night Jesus was betrayed is that scene on a road outside Rome, where an old and stumbling Peter is fleeing from the first political persecution of the Church. According to the legend, Peter meets Christ travelling the other way, going on to Rome. 'Quo vadis, Domine? Where are you going, Lord?' Peter asks. 'I'm going to Rome to die for you again.' No word of reproach. Just Christ the wayfarer, endlessly going up to Jerusalem to die. And Peter turned and went back to his own passion, and the tradition tells us, and it breaks the heart to think of it, that the old Jewish fisherman insisted on being crucified upside down because he was not worthy to die like his Lord.

No, Easter does not banish tragedy and suffering; it does not signal the end of all our striving, the drying of our tears. Instead, it takes us and shows us deep down into the heart of things where Christ is working his endless work of love. It shows us the triumph, the resurrection, that is laid in store for us *beyond* tragedy. On this day of waiting, this day after the struggle is over, this day of brimming regret, a sudden stillness falls upon the battlefield, for an instant the smoke clears. We catch sight of the high eternal hills; then the urgent thrill of a trumpet call, and there is Christ going before us, walking, walking on broken feet into the everlasting kingdom.

This death and its strange and glorious sequel do not banish tragedy. The world still suffers and grieves and regrets. But know that another thing is happening and this same tragedy, like Christ's wounds, is being transformed into a glory that gives it meaning beyond all our meanings in a time beyond all the time we know. In the words of Eliot's Becket:

'Peace, and be at peace with your thoughts and visions.
These things had to come to you and you accept them,
This is your share of the eternal burden,
The perpetual glory. This is one moment,
But know that another
Shall pierce you with a sudden painful joy
When the figure of God's purpose is made complete.
You shall forget these things, toiling in the household,
You shall remember them, droning by the fire,
When age and forgetfulness sweeten memory
Only like a dream that has often been told
And often been changed in the telling. They will seem unreal.
Human kind cannot bear very much reality.'

So this is one moment, but we also know another, yet not another, for it is the same moment in its truer meaning. That moment is the moment of Resurrection, which is the meaning of the death of Jesus from the side of God's purpose.

7. THE THIRD DAY

I have made large claims in this book for the death of Jesus. An event in history, it shows us something that is eternally true, it reveals to us something that lies behind all history. Like the ring of a tree which is exposed when the tree is cut, but which goes right through the tree, so is the human life of Jesus Christ. In that life, the very heart of God was exposed. God in Christ showed us what we could never have found out for ourselves: that he loves us so much that he suffers for us. The crucifixion of Jesus is not just an event in time: it is a showing-forth in time of something that is permanently true. Until the end of all ends when God's great struggle with Evil and Sorrow is concluded, there is a cross in the heart of God. But the death of Jesus Christ alone could not have told us that. His death was just another defeat, another failure—that is certainly how the principal actors in the drama of his death saw it. Like many another Messianic Pretender, Jesus of Nazareth would have sunk into oblivion and his poignant and heroic death would, like so many others, have gone unremembered—if he had not been raised from the dead on the third day. Everything I have written and everything that has ever been written about Jesus Christ, has been written *after* the Resurrection, and it is the Resurrection which controls the interpretation of everything that went before. It was the Resurrection which lifted the veil which had hung over the eyes of even his closest followers so that, at last, they *saw*. In other words, the Resurrection is the foundation stone of the Christian Faith—remove it and the whole thing collapses. Nothing else would have been remembered about this man, nothing would have been *worth* remembering, if he had not been raised from the dead. That is why, when his followers first surface in history they are even then preaching the Resurrection. So overwhelmed are they by the majesty and revolutionary power of that event, that they seem to pay little attention to other things we long to know! Paul is the great exemplar here: for him preaching Christ *was* preaching the Resurrection! So close is the identity between his preaching of Jesus and his preaching of the Resurrection that Luke tells us in the Acts of the

Apostles that the pagan philosophers who heard Paul preach thought he was proclaiming two gods: one called Jesus and the other called Anastasis or Resurrection.

When we think about the Resurrection we have to make a distinction between what happened and what it means; between the event and its significance. The closest we can get to what happened is the evidence supplied by the New Testament writers, the sworn testimony of his first followers. There is no other independent account of what occurred. The first witnesses tell us what they saw and experienced. Let us now turn to one of the accounts, to the twentieth chapter of the Gospel of John. John's Gospel is reckoned to be the latest of the Gospels, but it has long been held to have behind it the experience and memory of him who is known in the Gospel itself as 'the beloved disciple', John the Apostle. I see no persuasive reason to discount the tradition which believes that in this Gospel we are close to the experience, however it was subsequently interpreted, of an eyewitness and participant in the events it describes. The account of the Resurrection in John is simple, its meaning unmistakable. The dead body of Jesus had been laid in a tomb late on the Eve of the Passover. Nothing could be done to it, no visit made during the Passover Festival. Now the Passover is at an end and the first day of the week is here, though it is not yet dawn. The time is anywhere between three and five in the morning. Some women come to the tomb, though John, for his purposes, only names Mary Magdalene. She sees that the great stone has been rolled away from the tomb, and she immediately concludes that the body has been stolen. She runs to Peter, then to John, the beloved disciple, and tells them the situation.

They set out immediately in a race to the garden, but John, probably a much younger man, outruns Peter and gets there first. That's the kind of detail that suggests the eyewitness, now an old man, recalling every moment of that unforgettable morning, even the fact that once he could run like a deer! John does not go in to the tomb; he stoops and looks in and sees the winding-sheet lying empty. Peter arrives and characteristically dashes straight in and gazes carefully at the scene. John follows him in and the words he uses to describe the scene are careful and specific. There is no disarray in the tomb, no evidence of ransacking. The winding sheet lies there still in place, but empty. Even more specific, the napkin that went round the head lies a little apart, as would the head itself, and it is still wound like a turban (the Greek word is quite specific), but it is empty, too. In other words, the grave clothes are still in place as though they were round a body, except that they lie empty and deflated, flattened down upon themselves. We read that John saw all this 'and believed'.

These are either the careful details of an eyewitness, or the cunning fabrications of an impostor. John wants us to understand, quite clearly, that the tomb was empty and that his faith was a result of what he saw, and not the other way round. It is important to understand that. There are those who find it impossible to accept that there could have been such a thing as a resurrection. It has nothing to do with evidence. They are just not prepared to entertain the idea. They are locked into a world-view which precludes a supernatural divine intervention of this sort. They will not believe though one were to rise from the dead. People who are in this position have a problem with the New Testament, because it bears clear and embarrassing and concrete witness to the Resurrection. It is true that there is no mention of the empty tomb in Paul, and certain critics cling to this with desperate gratitude; but it is doubtful if Paul would understand the use they make of him. Paul is quite clear about the objectivity of the Resurrection, and goes into quite precise detail in his enumeration of the Resurrection appearances. Nowhere does he give an account of the event as made known to the apostles. He simply takes it for granted:

'I delivered to you as of first importance what I also received, that Christ died for our sins in accordance with the scriptures, that he was buried, that he was raised on the third day in accordance with the scriptures, and that he appeared to Cephas, then to the twelve. Then he appeared to more than five hundred brethren at one time, most of whom are still alive, though some have fallen asleep. Then he appeared to James, then to all the apostles. Last of all, as to one untimely born, he appeared also to me.' I Cor.15.3–8

The argument from silence is very flimsy, and lends itself to tendentious interpretation: if it suits the position you hold on other grounds, use it. A simple test will confirm this observation. Without taking sides on the issue, the arguments for and against the ordination of women to the priesthood provides an instructive illustration here. Both sides use the argument from silence in different ways. Those who are opposed to it offer the silence of scripture on the subject as argument; those in favour say, correctly I think, that you cannot derive a positive argument from an absence of fact. If there are grounds for the opposition to the ordination of women, they must be more positive than the argument from silence, otherwise the possibilities for negative projection are endless. No mention is made in scripture that our Lord called a baker to the apostleship. Does that rule out bakers? Nor does he call a Scottish apostle. Does that rule out Scots? You can prove nothing from something that is not mentioned. Paul does not mention the empty tomb, but the only conclusion we can draw from that is that he chose not to. There is undoubtedly a measure of irony in the fact that some of those who argue that the tomb could not have been empty because Paul does not mention it, are also those who pour most scorn upon the argument that there can be no ordination of women because the New Testament does not mention it.

The fact is, of course, that those who dismiss a corporeal or bodily resurrection do it on *a priori* grounds: it *could* not happen therefore it *did* not happen. They get round the problem presented by the New Testament's enthusiastic proclamation of the Resurrection by saying that the Resurrection was something that happened, not to Jesus, but to the apostles: faith rose up in them, their hope was rekindled, and that faith and that hope they wove into a story. Well, it seems to me to be more honest to call them liars or fools than to play that sort of game with their evidence. In a matter of hours they have been totally changed. They account for that revolution in their lives by saying it was caused by the Resurrection. They do not say that they found themselves changed, somehow, and decided, on that basis, that the death of Christ must have been reversed. It is very important to grasp this distinction. Something momentous happened, which changed the followers of Jesus from a bunch of dispirited deserters into one of the most remarkable bands of men and women whom history has produced. Do you accept the reasons they give for the change? *They* say he was raised from the dead in the totality of his being, including his body. The tomb was empty! The body was never produced! There was no trade in relics from his body. The body was gone and was never again produced, and John clearly wishes us to understand from his careful description of the grave clothes that some mysterious process had intervened. Now, I cannot say *what* happened to the corpse of Jesus in scientific terms, though it would appear to have something to do with the regeneration of matter. The closest I can come to any conceptualization of the event is this: the Christian believes that the physical universe came into existence as a result of a creative act of God. One way of putting this is to say that there was once a time when God existed and the universe did not; and that, from nothing but himself, God created matter, and the potency and energy we call the physical universe evolved from it. Once, there was nothing but God; then, there was God and the universe. The Resurrection seems to be a kind of reversion of that process, from one point of view. By another act of God, one handful of matter has been trans-materialized, transfigured, transposed to that original order of being we call Spirit which characterizes the nature of God. I cannot for the life of me tell how he did it, anymore than I can tell how he inaugurated matter in the first place, but the second miracle seems to me to be no more stupendous than the first. One reason I can accept the miracle of Resurrection is that I have come to terms with the miracle of Creation.

Many people find this hard to believe, I know. Well, let me say this. It is one thing to struggle and fail to cope with a majestic and mysterious claim like this one and say: 'I just don't know. I just can't bring myself to accept it, but I know in other ways that Jesus is alive, and I *want* to believe what the Church believes. So, please God, accept what I *can* believe and help what I can't!' That is honest, and there has always been very wide scope in the Christian Church for honest doubt of that sort. There is another step which is much more fateful. That step is taken when Christians try to manipulate the fundamentals of the Christian tradition to make them conform to their current thinking. Obviously, Christians have a permanent duty imposed upon them to translate the Christian message into understandable forms. But this permanent necessity is one that concerns *form*, not *substance*: it is translation, not radical rewriting. This is why it is exasperating to find scholars who say, not that the New Testament writers are lying, but that they mean the opposite of what they say! That is to read one's own presuppositions into the text. It is a very human thing to do. The trouble with it is that you can be so busy doing it, so busy trying to make the New Testament fit your own point of view, that you fail absolutely to hear what it has to say to *you*. Maybe by listening carefully, by opening ourselves to it, some of the things that happened to them can happen to us.

So let us ask what this strange event meant to the disciples and what it means to us. A moment's thought will provide a partial answer. Anyone who has lost someone they love knows the empty, painful, aching, unconsolable feeling that ensues. What's worst is that they are no longer *there*, but you are and you go on wanting to share things with them. At times you forget the reality of the situation and you say 'John will really enjoy that. I must tell him'. Then you realize that John cannot enjoy it with you any longer or give you the benefit of his thoughts, for he is no longer accessible, no longer with you. At this point, many people have recourse to a medium, desperate to get back into touch with someone they've lost. They may receive assurance of some sort, conviction about post-mortem survival, but it's not what they are really looking for. Many people try to make out that is what the disciples got, some kind of psychic telegram from The Other Side. Well, *they* say they got much more than that. They claim that they got him back totally, magnified a million times in glory and significance, so unlike the pathetic and dreary little messages that come through Spiritualism. That is the first thing it meant to them. It banished their grief entirely. He was still with them, and with them in a way that was much closer and more penetrating than when he was limited to his earthly life. The New Testament positively trumpets with the heart-bursting realization that he is not dead, but is alive for evermore! You can feel it as you study the pages: barely controllable grief, confronted with a truth that it dare not, cannot grasp. Then it is slowly invaded by light and certainty, peace and joy and that filling of the heart that sent them out to win everything for Christ. Jesus lives!

That is still the truth that Christians preach. I know he lives for I, too, have met him. Like Peter, I have been unfaithful to him. Like Thomas, I have doubted him. Like the two who walked disconsolately to Emmaus, I have been foolish and slow of heart to believe. Yet I know he is alive, and he has come to me as he came to them. Like Peter, I have felt his eyes gazing with terrible and burning love into my heart and I have gone out and wept bitterly because of what I have done: I have known him in conscience. Like Thomas, I have felt his presence close to me as I have prayed, and I have reached out my hands and sought to surrender myself and all my doubts: I have known him in prayer. Like Cleopas and his companion at nightfall in Emmaus, I have felt him draw close to me at the breaking of bread in Church: I have known him in sacrament. Conscience, prayer, sacrament: these are but three ways in which he comes to us still, and there are many, many more.

Jesus lives! That is the first meaning of the Resurrection. He is not entombed on a Galilean hillside or between the pages of a book we long to but cannot believe; or in the experience of people holier than ourselves, but alive and accessible to us, if we will but seek after him. That is the first meaning of the Resurrection, and this is the second.

'You now therefore have sorrow', said Jesus to his disciples before he was taken from them in death. Sorrow is the mark of man in so many ways. There is the sorrow of death, the sorrow of loss, the sorrow the disciples would know at his death. The Resurrection, as we have seen, overcame that specific sorrow. But there is another kind of sorrow which is not yet overcome. It is what Hopkins called 'a chief woe, world-sorrow', the sorrow that lies at the heart of all things as they change and fade and sink inexorably into the past. This day, with all its secrets and its joys vividly present to us, will one day be the past, and people will strive to understand what it could have been like back in 1979. Think of all the unknown men and women in all the unnumbered back streets in all the towns that ever were! It is impossible for the Christian priest to forget the words of Isaiah: 'All flesh is grass'. Even if he is sometimes tempted to forget his own mortality, his job endlessly confronts him with the mortality of others.

I have been in Old St Paul's Church in Edinburgh for only ten years, yet already I have officiated at hundreds of funerals. Hundreds of times have I led a coffin down the Calvary Stairs with the Nunc Dimittis on my lips: 'Lord, now lettest thou thy servant depart in peace.' And there have been times when I have never wanted to do it again. There have been times when I have never again wanted to be ushered into one of those long, black cars and move off under the Scotsman Bridge, as another member of my congregation is taken on their last journey to their long home. There have been times when the dominion of death has suffocated me with anguish and uncertainty, *because their names are all written down*! We have bound volumes of the names of those who have gone down into the grave. Thousands of names. An entry for each life, reduced at last to a scrawl of ink on paper:

'Buried 10th December 1893: Jane McLeish, 17 Borthwick's Close, aged 5 years.
'Buried 16th May 1914: Robert Brown, 111 Pleasance, aged 43 years.
Buried 16th January 1975: Muriel Robson, 10 Warrender Park Terrace, aged 70 years.'

I often think of the strange, hurting wistfulness of it all: all those glad lives and dancing feet, all gone down into the grave. But the thing that most wounds me is not their dying. It is not their dying, for that at least is recorded, is written down. What despairs me is their living, their *unremembered* living. I grieve for all those lives which are unrecalled. Someone once said that every person has at least one book in him, the story of his own life. Every life is filled with incident and quiet heroism, with struggle and joy. I can go to the library and get out the life of Lord Curzon. I can find out nothing about Robert Brown of 111, Pleasance, died in 1914 aged 43. And think of the millions of whom that can be said! As one contemplates the teeming prodigality of human history, one is tempted to meaninglessness at the thought of all that being born and going down into death. The endless endingness of everything. 'You now therefore have sorrow', sorrow because you can discern no meaning, no end to this insatiable universe which devours time and all its children. It *is* meaningless, without the Resurrection. By the taking of Christ into glory, God has given us a glimpse of his plan for his universe. He has, in Paul's words, let us in on his own secret purpose which is to reverse the inexorable process of decay, the running-down of the universe, and to establish all things in Christ in a new creation that will know no more dying or separation, nor any tears but those of joy. And we could never have figured this out for ourselves! We know these things only because the love of God has made them known to our hearts by his revelation of himself in Jesus Christ.

What, then, is left for us to do? Do we just wait for the return of Christ who is present in a hidden manner in the folds of history? ·Yes and no. Yes and no, because while he is glorified and has taken our dust into heaven, we are still caught in the dialectic of the dust we are· and the glory that awaits us. On one level, the mystery of Christ is what Mother Julian would call a Showing, an exhibition, an unveiling of what is even now coming to pass. Beneath the agony and decay of the universe, God is at work restoring it, reintegrating it into its destiny. This is the mystery with which Teilhard wrestled, and which called from him that baffling and poetic vision of a great process of cosmic transformation which is even now moving ineluctably towards its end. 'Step by step it irresistibly invades the universe. It is the fire that sweeps over the heath; the stroke that vibrates through the bronze' (de Chardin). Yes, this dust is bound for glory. Everything, every wounded child and every sparrow that falls to the ground in the cold of winter is, even now, being glorified. The Church exists to point men and women to the reality of what is happening now. As the old negro spiritual puts it: 'We're on the road to glory.' There is nothing else to say in Auschwitz or in the terminal ward of the cancer hospital or by the graveside on a dark Friday afternoon. There is only that. And if we felt it, if we knew it, 'it would bring back the whole world'. Those who have been let in on the secret of the ages glow with the knowledge. The glory of that Kingdom casts its brightness back into time and illumines the faces that look towards it. 'For it is the God who said, "Let light shine out of darkness", who has shone in our hearts to give the light of the knowledge of the glory of God in the face of Christ.' (2 Cor.4.6)

This, then, is the final meaning of the Resurrection of Jesus Christ from the dead: it is a preview of the great future that awaits the whole of the created universe. That is why all the Easter hymns say that the Resurrection destroys death and sorrow, even 'world-sorrow', and bids our hearts rise with Christ.

> 'Can there be any day but this,
> Though many suns to shine endeavour?
> We count three hundred, but we miss:
> There is but one, and that one ever.'
>
> George Herbert.

PART 2

You are the body of Christ: that is to say,
in you and through you the work of the
Incarnation must go forward. You are meant
to incarnate in your lives the theme of your
adoration—you are to be taken, consecrated,
broken and distributed, that you may be the means
of grace and vehicles of the Eternal Charity.

St Augustine

8. LONGING

The whisky priest in Graham Green's novel, *The Power and the Glory*, sits in a prison cell the night before his execution and mourns the waste he has made of his life. It seems to him that, somewhere in the past, he missed happiness 'by seconds at an appointed place'. It's a phrase that has haunted me for years, because it suggests both movements in the drama of man's losing or finding God. It all happens at an appointed place, ordained by God. One thing is central to everything I have written so far: God comes in search of us. He has been drawing us to himself from all eternity: 'Yea, I have loved thee with an everlasting love and with cords of love I have drawn thee.' God has a permanent appointment with man. He waits for us. Why, then, do we miss the appointment, more often than not? If God is really searching for us, why do we miss him so often? I suspect that it is all a matter of momentary but fateful inattention. We constantly miss him by seconds at all his appointed places. Intentionally? Perhaps. Yet, all the time we are searching for him. God in search of man. Man in search of God. How is the connection made? Until the connection is made, until the appointment is kept, God cannot rest and we cannot be happy.

In Part 1, I described God's love seeking us out in Christ, coming after us to the very depths. In this part, I want to suggest ways in which we might keep the appointment God constantly makes for us. I want to suggest ways in which we might make the connection between his search and ours. Why bother? Because we only know real happiness when we keep that appointment made for us from all eternity. If we miss it, as we do so often, we experience a mysterious sense of loss. Make no mistake, behind the brave fronts and the cheerful faces that many people put on, there often lies a great deal of heartbreak and dissatisfaction. Sometimes the reasons for this are obvious: they are caused by the objective tragedies of life, tragedies which can and do strike anywhere, anyhow. But most people are hardly able to identify the unease that afflicts them. Their lives, they feel, have not turned out quite the way they wanted them to. They sense, deep within themselves,

sleeping powers and gifts and potentialities that have never
been properly expressed. They feel vague and unsatisfied hungers, strange longings for a joy they have never known, yet
long for. Most of us, I suspect, have felt something of this. If
you've lived for any time at all; if your face is at all worn by
time and your heart battered by chance, then you will admit
that there is a strange, aching gap between what you are and
what you once longed to be. You may explain it to yourself
by saying that you never got the breaks you deserved. You are
locked in by the constraints of circumstances and the responsi-
bilities of your state to a way of life that does not fully express your own secret desires. Edwin Muir described the state
in these words:

'I am astonished by the contrast between the powers I am
aware of in me and the triteness of my life. As I grow older
I feel more and more the need to make that barren astonishment effectual, to wrest some palpable prize from it; for I
cannot see that the astonishment itself is of any use to me.
I have a body, affections, desires, needs, like all men. I lead
in essentials much the same life. My time is spent in the
routine of sleeping, eating, working, and sleeping again. I
say the same things as everyone else, am daily troubled by
the same cares, perform the same actions, the actions which
keep us alive. There is nothing extraordinary in all this. But
when I turn to the thoughts and images in my mind—I admit
I do this only at exceptional moments—what a difference.
What an unbelievable difference.' (Autobiography)

Most people know the 'unbelievable difference' Edwin Muir
confided to his journal. It is the difference between the mag-
nificence of our longing and the mediocrity of our lives. It is
that difference, the difference we all know in our own lives,
that leads to cynicism, or that depression and despair which
is the Black Plague of our era. And even if we are fortunate
by the standards men set, even if we manage to snatch a few
of life's glittering prizes, how quickly they tarnish and become
dull, and off we go again on that strange pursuit for we know
not what. And we'll go anywhere to find what we're looking
for. You can define the whole of mankind's history and the
culture he has created, in all its wonderful richness, as the
result of this strange and endless quest. Even his most wonderful discoveries in art and his deepest experiences of love are,
finally, unable to bear the full weight of his longing. What he

is looking for is never completely within them, it only shines through them, tantalizing him again to continue the search for the light that never was on sea or land. All we get are glimpses, now and then, of the shadow which turns the corner always a pace or two ahead of us. In *Brideshead Revisited*, Evelyn Waugh caught the transient, wistful quality of all our earthly loves:

> 'Perhaps all our loves are merely hints and symbols; vagabond language scrawled on gate-posts and paving-stones along the weary road that others have tramped before us; perhaps you and I are types and this sadness which sometimes falls between us springs from disappointment in our search, each straining through and beyond the other, snatching a glimpse now and then of the shadow which turns the corner always a pace or two ahead of us.'

Is that all that can be said, then? Are we afflicted with an appetite than can never be satisfied, born with a longing that can never be fulfilled? Many there are who answer 'yes'. We are orphaned in a universe that has no father, and we had better get used to the pain. They tell us naught for our comfort. They call us, instead, to that defiant courage which endures the anguish, the anguish of those who long for the God they know does not exist. And there's more heroism and truth in that attitude than in much that passes for faith. You can almost divide humanity into those who are still looking for God and those who are consoling themselves because they know he does not exist. We dare not condemn mankind in its search for solace and escape, either. Too often the Church has set itself up as a universal scold to those who are merely seeking some temporary relief from the emptiness inside them, some brief joy before they go hence and be no more seen. The only appropriate response to the world's tormented search for consolation is a terrible pity. Any comfort will serve in a whirlwind, and which of us has not, at some time or other, sought relief from the incurable pain that afflicts us? Children lost in a dark wood are to be pitied, not condemned. Are we, then, utterly lost? There are those who search and do not seem able to find, and those who have given up the search because they have decided it is futile. What else can be said?

St Augustine is the great poet and theologian of this everlasting longing which troubles man. We are looking, longing, waiting for God, and nothing that is not God will satisfy the

God-need. Meanwhile, we hunger and we yearn, we look up and are not fed. We are afflicted with this longing, says Augustine, our hearts are never at rest, not because what we long for does not exist, but because we once knew it and have wandered from it and have forgotten how to return. Mankind is in the far-country of exile from the Father he is born remembering, yet cannot find by searching. In his *Confessions* Augustine draws a helpful analogy from the activity of thinking and remembering. The very word re-member suggests a bringing back together of broken and forgotten fragments into their original unity, and this is the very activity we call thinking. We take things which the memory already contains, but which are scattered and un-arranged, and by thinking, bring them together, and by close attention have them placed within reach in that same memory. So thinking is an activity of collecting together and making unities of fragmented and partial truths, rather like the piecing of a jigsaw together. This is why we are able to recognize and approve when a 'new' idea is put to us. We say, 'that's right! Why didn't *I* think of that before?' We recognize the truth when it is put back together, very much as we assent to the placing of difficult yet appropriate pieces in a jigsaw, because it is a pattern we know, though we may not know why.

We encounter the same phenomenon among many creative artists. They do not claim that their work is theirs in an originative sense. They are mid-wives who assist the poem or the painting or the symphony to be born. Let me illustrate that with the story of a remarkable man. Osip Mandelstam was one of the finest Russian poets of this century. One day, he wrote a witty little four-line lampoon on Stalin which was passed hastily from hand to hand like a time-bomb in a parcel. One day it was passed on to Stalin himself, and he hunted Mandelstam to death, playing with him the way a well-fed cat plays with a mouse—with a bored, almost absent-minded cruelty. Mandelstam was killed in 1938. A few years ago his wife produced a remarkable book called *Hope Against Hope*, in which she described their life together during those heroic last years when the man in the Kremlin played out his game against her gentle and unworldly husband. She preserved his poetry by memory, and describes how it circulated in the underground of Russian society, passed from hand to hand scribbled on old envelopes and grubby scraps of paper. It was one of the most amazing adventures of the human spirit. In a fascinating passage she describes how her husband wrote his poetry. He did not sit down and think it up, dredging it out of his own mind. It came to him from outside, like a signal, faint at first, then getting louder till it came over with unavoidable clarity. For him, writing a poem was an act of listening, of awareness, in which he strained to *hear* the message and get it down on paper. He was the sensitive and willing instrument, cooperating with the poem, helping it like a good mid-wife, to be born. The poem had an independent existence of its own.

I have discovered the same method in other poets. They feel that the poem has an independent existence; they do not create or compose it. It comes *through* them. The Scottish poet, Edwin Muir, describes his poetic activity as an attempt to remember and record that other world, eternal, original, unchangeably and heartbreakingly beautiful, which lies behind this world of change and chance which we inhabit. All of us come from that world, however you name it, and we are haunted by it and its remembrance bursts into our conscious mind from time to time if we'll let it, and into our dreams whether we'll let it or not. We are like the man who has lost his memory, yet who is tormented by fleeting and unconnected remembrances of his former life. Many artists, poets and musicians have interpreted their work in this way. Their activity is an activity of listening or looking. We are all born trying to remember where we came from. Most of us are brainwashed out of that act of remembering, today. For several generations, our map of reality has been rigidly empirical. We are taught that only reason can put us in touch with what is real. No other reality than that which is accessible to reason can be said to exist. The windows of perception which open onto the other world we long for, have been blacked-out. The fascinating lore of those who have searched for that other world has been systematically denigrated. Fortunately, there have always been men and women who have kept in close touch with that other world, in spite of the ridicule and prohibitions and persecutions of fashionable tyrannies. They have allowed that other world to break into this world through them. They have kept the rumour of its existence alive.

One of the fascinating ironies of our era is that, in spite of a century or so of withering opposition from the opinion-formers of the cultural and philosophical Establishment, men and women of our day are embarking on an enthusiastic search for 'the other country'. In their search, they are combing the old maps and guides of every generation, ransacking the storerooms of ancient religions and following the nostrums of contemporary guides. Theodore Roszak has called this loose, sprawling and animated religious revival in Western society, 'the Aquarian frontier'. He says this about it:

'... we find in this rising curiosity for the marvellous, the popular unfolding of an authentically spiritual quest, which has been driven into a variety of unorthodox channels by the rigidity of conventional religion in the Western world. While that quest has yet to develop the discriminating taste it will require if it is to endure and flourish, its emergence is the necessary and healthy sign of spiritual resurgence.'

The experience of today's new searchers for the old wisdom, and the experience of artists down the centuries, are partially corroborated by the researchers of Carl Jung who claimed that men and women are not born into this world as empty vessels waiting to be impressed and formed only by experience in this life. They come already 'trailing clouds of glory', in Wordsworth's phrase. They come already wistful and haunted by memories and dreams and unconsolable longings. They are born searching for a lost happiness. But the happiness is not utterly lost, it is only buried, like the truth, within our fragmented selves. So we are empty, waiting to be filled; lost, waiting to be found. St Augustine knew all this from his own experience.

'... where in my memory dost thou abide, O Lord? Where dost thou dwell there? What sort of lodging hast thou made for thyself there? ... place there is none. We go backward and forward and there is no place. Everywhere and at once, O Truth, thou guidest all who consult thee, and simultaneously answerest all, even though they consult thee on quite different things ... Late have I loved thee, O Beauty so ancient and so new, late have I loved thee. For see, thou wast within and I was without, and I sought thee out there. Unlovely, I rushed heedlessly among the lovely things thou hast made. Thou wast with me, but I was not with thee. These things kept me far from thee; even though they were not at all unless they were in thee.'

Two things impede our search for the beauty that haunts us. The first is dread. We are more than half afraid of the consequences of really finding God, 'Lest, having Him, I must have naught beside'. So we search with a sort of studious absent-mindedness. Freud talked about people who left things in other people's houses, conveniently if unconsciously losing them there so that they can find an excuse for going back again. With God we do the opposite of that. We busy ourselves in an apparently sincere search for him, but in fact we are desperately keen not to find him, so we make sure we don't look too closely in areas where we might find him. But the second impediment is an absolutely proper sense that no man, by searching *can* find out God. He either forms idols in his own image, projections of his own need or vanity, or he rests humbly in the knowledge of his own powerlessness. He is at the point of faith when he realizes the collapse of all his own proud efforts. What he once failed to achieve by will, he might now receive by grace, for it is the fundamental insight of the Gospel, rediscovered by Augustine, that *we* do not find God; he finds us in our lostness.

'Thou didst call and cry aloud, and didst force open my deafness. Thou didst gleam and shine, and didst chase away my blindness. Thou didst breathe fragrant odours and I drew in my breath; and now I pant for thee. I tasted, and now I hunger and thirst. Thou didst touch, and I burned for thy peace.' Confessions.

The Christian Church does not offer men and women a route-map to God. Instead, it tells them by what means they might be found by him! The emphasis is always upon God's initiative. When Peter blurts out his confession of faith in Christ at Caesarea Philippi, Jesus, according to Matthew, tells him that 'flesh and blood has not revealed this to you, but my Father in heaven'. The same point is made in John's Gospel when Jesus tells the Jews: 'No one can come to me unless the Father who sent me draws him.' And most of the parables of Jesus emphasize the activity of God in his search for mankind. He comes after us like a shepherd searching for his lost sheep; like a woman sweeping her room till she finds her lost coin; like the waiting father who sees his lost son while he is yet a great way off and runs towards him, with tears on his cheek and in total disregard of common prudence and worldly justice, to embrace him and bring him back home. The Christian doctrine of the Incarnation gathers this theme into one arresting proclamation which asserts that God himself has come after us by submitting to our nature and its limitations in the person of Jesus. And this is not just an assertion about history, about what happened in the past: he came *then*. The Letter to the Hebrews tells us that 'Jesus Christ is the same yesterday and today and forever'. He is the everlasting contemporary, equidistant from all history, able to be known today. The Church's proclamation sums this doctrine up in the simple claim, 'Jesus Lives!' We are not just the guardians of a form of words which enshrines that claim. We are witnesses to an experience that validates the claim, and it is this which we invite others to share. We claim that the presence of Christ can be experienced now, is a present fact. According to John's Gospel, Jesus told his disciples that the Holy Spirit would be with them for ever, to guide them into the dynamic truth of Christ, a truth which would follow each generation of Christians and be available to them with the same vividness and certainty as was present in the Upper Room.

One of the greatest tragedies of Christian history has been the subtle process by which the Christian Church has come to be seen as the protectress of a sealed and rigid list of doctrinal formulae. The only life which seems to surround this custodial role is the periodic outbreak of intellectual warfare between theologians as to the precise meaning of the documents safely stored in the ecclesiastical vaults. We are enduring one of these scholarly uproars at the moment. Forgotten is the recognition that we are talking about a contemporary! Theologians tend to behave as though Jesus were well and truly dead, so that his words and deeds and the interpretation surrounding them are now a permanent hunting ground for scholarly abstraction. The central Christian claim is that he still lives and is therefore accessible to us both for the living of our own lives and for guidance in the interpretation of his. We are not squabbling over the will of a dead relative. We are in the presence of the living Lord of life.

Let me conclude this chapter by gathering together what I have tried to say. I have no statistical data to support the claim, but I believe that most men and women have a God-hunger, which is often deeply repressed, but which shows itself in a prevailing sense of personal dissatisfaction. One way of explaining this would be to say that our frustration arises because we have an appetite for the Absolute and the Final and none of the things we find in life is Absolute and Final, though we sometimes try to impose an absolute value upon them.

The technical word for this is 'idolatry' and it is an unavoidable human activity. We have a need to find absolute value but we cannot find any object, any person that deserves it, so we impose it upon substitutes. The heart-breaking and often beautiful thing about human culture is that it is evidence of our orphaned search for a place to belong, but is itself unable to bear the full weight of our longing. The Christian Gospel recognizes all of us, but it begins with the recognition that no effort on humanity's part will resolve the fundamental problem: we are without God in the world, yet we have a deep and inneffaceable natural longing for him. The Gospel, however, witnesses to the fact that God himself has come in search of us! He finds us in our need and makes himself known. This is the meaning of Jesus Christ, who was the presence of God yesterday and is still that presence today and will be that presence for ever. It is to that simple and scandalous claim the Church witnesses. It points to the living Christ. But it does more. It shows men and women a way by which they might be found of Christ. There is, in the Christian tradition, millennia of spiritual experience. This practical guidance can be used now as a way for today. This book has been written in the hope that it might be of help to some of those who are looking for the way.

9. RESPONDING

The teachers and spiritual guides of any of the great religions know that there can be no real progress in the spiritual life, no increase in the knowledge of God, unless there is some direct personal experience or communion with the divine. Without this experiential element, religion becomes abstract and formal, as has been the case with Western Christianity for centuries. Religion that lacks this personal dimension does not wear well, and cannot stand up to the pressures and erosions of the surrounding culture. When the surrounding culture, for one reason or another, 'establishes' religion, it may endure for entirely social or cultural reasons, but in the time of testing it collapses, for it is built on no solid ground. One of the reasons for the alleged decline of religion in the West is surely attributable to this lack of a vivid, personal experience in the lives of most people. It is significant, therefore, that, while 'formal' religion continues to decline, there has been a dramatic resurgence of experiential religion in the West, and by no means all of it has been Christian. Every Western city will testify to the presence of strange, esoteric religions in its midst, offering a way through the mazes of the mind to a direct communion with the divine.

It is significant that many of today's seekers pass the Christian Church by without a thought, persuaded that it no longer has any spiritual experience to offer, that it has been utterly emptied of the divine madness. Equally significant is the fact that those parts of the Christian Church which continue to grow and attract new seekers after God, offer a vividly experiential religion. This is the significance of the neo-Charismatic Movement in all the mainline Churches in the West. Men and women, in the depths of their heart, are no longer greatly interested in a religious tradition that tells them 'about' God but can offer no guidance towards achieving communion 'with' God. By that strange economy of the divine mercy, it is entirely appropriate that at a time of great spiritual aridity, there has emerged a great religious movement, spanning all the Christian traditions and creating unity between them, which offers an experience of the divine life, a direct involvement in that reality we all long to discover. Its greatest triumph lies in the simple fact that it has made people expectant again. It has shown them that God still makes himself known to man, and that he comes to them in flames of joy and wonder. Small wonder, therefore, that there has broken out, even in the stuffiest churches, a sense of supernatural expectation which, though frequently uncritical in its interpretation of what is happening, is giving people a sense of the accessibility of God.

The fact is, of course, that many men and women have left testimony concerning their experience of the divine, their communion with that reality which is the source and satisfaction of the longing that afflicts us. In an age when there has been a determined effort to remove every rumour of the divine from life, these witnesses have not been listened to, but their words abide and they call to us. I want to quote from three of them, and then give the results of a very remarkable survey which was carried out recently in the United States of America on the same subject.

My first example is the most famous. It is the note made by Blaise Pascal on the night he experienced the reality of the divine life.

> 'From about half past ten in the evening to
> about half an hour after midnight.
> Fire.
> God of Abraham, God of Isaac, God of Jacob,
> Not the God of philosophers and scholars.
> Absolute Certainty: Beyond reason.
> Joy. Peace.
> Forgetfulness of the world and everything but God.
> The world has not known thee, but I have known thee.
> Joy! Joy! Joy! tears of joy!'

My second example comes from the well-known writer on mysticism, F. C. Happold.

'It happened in my room in Peterhouse on the evening of February 1st, 1913, when I was an undergraduate at Cambridge. If I say that Christ came to me I should be using conventional words which would carry no precise meaning; for Christ comes to men and women in different ways. When I tried to record the experience at the time, I used the imagery of the vision of the Holy Grail; it seemed to me to be like that. There was, however, no sensible vision. There was just the room, with its shabby furniture and the fire burning in the grate and the red-shaded lamp on the table. But the room was filled by a Presence, which in a strange way was both about me and within me, like light or warmth. I was overwhelmingly possessed by Someone who was not myself, and yet I felt I was more myself than I had ever been before. I was filled with an intense happiness, and almost unbearable joy, such as I had never known before and have never known since. And over all was a deep sense of peace and security and certainty.'

My final example comes from Edwin Muir, the Scottish poet whom I have already quoted. Just before the Second World War he lived at St Andrews. He was dogged by darkness and despair and a sense of uselessness. He had long given up the practices of religion. His burden grew heavier when his wife fell ill and had to go into a nursing home. These words are taken from his autobiography.

'I was returning from the nursing home one day—it was the last day of February 1939—when I saw some schoolboys playing at marbles on the pavement; the old game had "come round" again at its own time, known only to children, and it seemed a simple little rehearsal for a resurrection, promising a timeless renewal of life. I wrote in my diary next day: "Last night, going to bed alone, I suddenly found myself (I was taking off my waistcoat) reciting the Lord's Prayer in a loud, emphatic voice—a thing I had not done for many years—with deep urgency and profound disturbed emotion. While I went on I grew more composed; as if it had been empty and craving and were being replenished, my soul grew still; every word had a strange fullness of meaning which astonished and delighted me. It was late; I had sat up reading; I was sleepy; but as I stood in the midst of the floor half-undressed, saying the prayer over and over, meaning after meaning sprang from it, overcoming me again with joyful surprise; and I realized that this simple petition was always universal and always inexhaustible, and day by day sanctified human life." '

Andrew M. Greely, the programme director of the Centre for the Study of American Pluralism at the National Opinion Research Centre, University of Chicago, and William C. McGready, the associate programme director, discovered, almost by accident that a number of people they knew had had experiences like the ones described by Pascal, Happold and Muir. They managed to find room in 'a representative national survey of ultimate values among some 1,500 American adults for a handful of questions on mystical experiences'. They were staggered by the response. 'About 600 persons—two-fifths of the 1,500 persons asked the question—reported having at least one such experience.' Intrigued, they went further with the research in an attempt to identify the kind of person who was having this experience. This is their report.

'Who are the ones who have "mystical" experiences? People in their 40s and 50s are somewhat more likely to report "mystical" interludes than those in their 70s or their teens. Protestants are more likely to experience them than Jews, and Jews more likely than Catholics. Within the Protestant denominations, it is not the fundamentalists who are the most frequent "mystics" but the Episcopalians (more than half of them). And within the two major denominational groups, the Irish are more likely than their co-religionists (be they Protestant or Catholic) to be mystical. Who are those who have these episodes often? They are disproportionately male, disproportionately black, disproportionately college-educated, disproportionately above the $10,000 a year income level, and disproportionately Protestants.'

The directors of the survey found no evidence to indicate that the subjects of these experiences were socially or psychologically disturbed. They administered a test called the Psychological Well-being Scale, developed by Professor Norman Bradburn. The relationship between frequent ecstatic experiences and psychological well-being was the highest, according to Bradburn, ever recorded with his scale. The directors of the survey were faced with total and unreasoning opposition from their professional colleagues in the social-science establishment. They report:

'We confess to being somewhat dismayed when professional colleagues dismiss our findings with an abrupt certainty: "Those people can't be having religious experiences." Maybe not, but they're having something, and whatever the hell it is they are having, it correlates with mental health at a very high level. If we had found any other correlate, the mental-health establishment would be knocking down our doors demanding to know more. If anything else but "ecstasy" were that good for you, it would sell as if it wouldn't be on the market next year.'

Anyone who marches to the drumbeat of those critics who deny the reality of the kind of experiences I have quoted, or who are prone to dismiss without further thought the discoveries made by Greely and McGready, need read no further in this book. I am persuaded, both by my own experiences, and by what I have read, as well as by the tradition of spirituality to which I belong, that God goes in search of us and that he can be known now. Our longing to know the Eternal Beauty that haunts us is not illusory, but the weight of our dull nature holds us back. St Augustine, again, captures this better than anyone: 'I was swept up to thee by thy beauty and torn away from thee by my own weight.' We feel there is something drawing us away, yet here we are like some deep sea diver weighed down, rooted to the spot at the bottom of the ocean. Or to change the image from flight to fire, we feel that we want to catch fire, be enflamed and consumed by God's love, but the fire does not strike. To those who are in this situation, the Christian tradition offers Christ as the Way. He is the one who shows us the way to God, and as we travel that way we find that we are in him, that he *is* the way we travel. This is a divine riddle which cannot be explained. It can only be experienced, known from within, like the answer to the question of the Zen master, 'What is the sound of one hand clapping?'

Christians have found that their way to the Father lies through Christ. What is that way? It is the way of sacrifice and its symbol for Christians is the Eucharist. Here is St Augustine again:

'You are the body of Christ: that is to say, in you and through you the work of the Incarnation must go forward. You are meant to incarnate in your lives the theme of your adoration—you are to be taken, consecrated, broken and distributed, that you may be the means of grace and vehicles of the Eternal Charity'.

This quotation from Augustine is a profound theological pun in which three elements interweave. Behind it, at the most obvious level, is the experience of the Christian Eucharist, in which we take, bless, break and distribute the holy bread. But the Eucharist is not a pious little play we put on in church to remind us of the Last Supper. The bread and wine which are transmuted, transformed into the presence of Christ, localize and fix for our senses the eternal action of God in giving his Son for the life of the world. He is eternally taken, blessed, broken and given up for us. And we are to be taken into that Way, because it is the eternal rhythm of the soul's movement to God: it must be taken and consecrated, broken and distributed if it is to find God and rest in his. will. If we would really be found by God, therefore, we must let ourselves be taken; we must allow ourselves to be consecrated; we must prepare ourselves to be broken; and we must suffer ourselves to be given away. That is the Christian Way, and Christ warned us that it was narrow and little-travelled upon, yet it is the royal road to God. I want to use the four-fold pattern of sacrifice as the broad outline of a programme of spiritual formation or discipline, not in order that we might train ourselves to be 'spiritual', but in order that God might find us and give us what we crave but are unable to achieve by ourselves.

Like Christ, then, we must allow ourselves *to be taken*. The baptism of Jesus by John the Baptist can be interpreted as the historical moment when he demonstrated the surrender of himself to the will of God. In Jesus, that surrender was a permanent thing, the consistent and steady abandonment of his will to the Father. That was why the early Church was reluctant to accept the obvious meaning of Christ's submission to a baptism of repentance. John, we read in Matthew, was extremely reluctant to baptize one whose life denied the need of the ceremony to which he was submitting.

'Then Jesus came from Galilee to the Jordan to John, to be baptized by him. John would have prevented him, saying, I need to be baptized by you, and do you come to me? But Jesus answered him, "Let it be so now; for thus it is fitting for us to fulfill all righteousness." Then he consented.' (Matt. 3.13-15)

Was this quite specific act an important symbolic occasion for Jesus, which represented a decisive movement in his doing of the Father's will? No matter what the steady direction of the will may be, human beings need occasions in which they can express and make visible their interior commitment. The baptism to which he submitted, therefore, was an acting-out of the interior surrender of himself. And this must certainly be our pattern, however problematic it may be in the life of

Jesus. Before God can take us and use us we must offer ourselves, make ourselves available. There has to be a letting-go,
a moment which expresses and reinforces our soul's surrender
to God. Being the kind of creatures we are, there has to be
some symbolic gesture, some act, some moment that commits
us to 'the high austere and lonely way the spirit moves in'. Our
nature, when we leave it alone, recognizes this very well.
Humankind has always 'acted-out' all the moments that make
life significant. We have an instinct for ceremony which owes
its origin to the sacramental complexity of reality. We are not
just souls *with* bodies, we are embodied-souls, spiritual-bodies,
integrated realities, so that the outward expresses and reinforces the inward, and the inward gives meaning and power
to the outward expression. Why else do we make 'occasions'
of the important moments of our lives, whether 'secular' or
'religious'? There is a wintry kind of spirituality which disapproves of this instinct for play and ceremony, but it is
dangerously repressive of a natural need and seems to contradict the very nature of God, who himself clothed the creative
thought of his mind in all the garments of creation.

> 'Is it not by his high superfluousness we know
> Our God? For to equal a need
> Is natural, animal, mineral: but to fling
> Rainbows over the rain,
> And beauty above the moon, and secret rainbows
> On the domes of deep sea-shells,
> And make the necessary embrace of breeding
> Beautiful also as fire,
> Not even the weeds to multiply without blossom
> Nor the birds without music ...
> The extravagant kindness of God.' (Robinson Jeffers).

The impulse to celebrate life by art and music and liturgy and
dance is part of our very likeness to God, who set the stars in
their courses at the foundation of the world and all the sons
of God shouted for joy.

We are called, therefore, to some ceremony of surrender, a
moment in which we *express* our abandonment to God. The
moment of surrender can take any form, but it will be a form
that is appropriate to our condition, and there will be a certain
element of divine humour in it. The story of Naaman the
Syrian general provides us with an appropriate commentary
here. He came to Elisha to be healed of his leprosy, drawing

up at the prophet's door with his impressive entourage. Elisha did not even bother to go out to meet him!

> 'And Elisha sent a messenger to him, saying, "Go and wash in the Jordan seven times, and your flesh shall be restored, and you shall be clean". But Naaman was angry, and went away, saying, "Behold, I thought that he would surely come out to me, and stand, and call on the name of the Lord his God, and wave his hand over the place, and cure the leper. Are not Abana and Pharpar, the rivers of Damascus, better than all the waters of Israel? Could I not wash in them, and be clean?" So he turned and went away in a rage. But his servants came near and said to him, "My father, if the prophet had commanded you to do some great thing, would you not have done it? How much rather, then, when he says to you, "Wash and be clean"? So he went down and dipped himself seven times in the Jordan, according to the word of the man of God; and his flesh was restored like the flesh of a little child, and he was clean.' 2 Kings 5.10-14

There is usually some carefully guarded no-entry zone which has to be breached within us, some proud tower which has to be torn down. As it was for Naaman, the moment of surrender may have to be intrinsically demeaning or humbling. The pride of intellect, some reserve or polite control of our nature, some carefully formed attitude: whatever it is, it has to go and cast itself into the muddy Jordan. And because we can only be truly taken if we are truly offered, the surrender of ourselves must be unconditional; there must be no small print at the bottom of the page which qualifies everything.

The exasperating thing about all this, is that this is no once-for-all event. Having made an absolute fool of ourselves down there in the water in front of all those people, we realize that it is but a beginning. Even for Jesus the event was a symbol of a process, the constant giving of the will to God. The will is not a static object, like an electrical appliance, which can be handed over once-and-for-all. The will is a dynamic force, and surrendering it is an endlessly repeated activity. The baptism, the moment of offering and being taken, is the emblem or sign of a process that is never complete but is now to be inaugurated. The reason for this lies in the nature of the self. The self is a magnetic, centripetal force, pulling in towards itself all the time, forming the self into a dense, hard ball, carefully protected and insulated. This is the permanent tendency of the self which is never effectively controlled. The shift of emphasis from the self to God is a permanent activity. Conversion is not a single event, even for those who've had dramatic spiritual experiences of the sort described at the beginning of this chapter. Conversion is a dynamic activity in which the soul is slowly unselfed and remade, formed after the pattern of Jesus. It has to have a beginning, and the beginning is of enormous importance.

The 'moment' we allow ourselves to be taken by God is the entry into a process. It means that the self must learn a double activity of awareness: acute awareness of and attention towards God and towards the neighbour. We have embarked upon a prising of the self from the self. The self is like one of those animals who curl up and contract into a defensive ball in the face of threat. We are going to unwind that little ball of quivering and irritable fear and open it out, turn its attention outwards, away from its own problems and joys, and point it towards God. The other word for this process of attention is 'prayer'. Prayer is the attentive application of the soul to God, the making of the soul ready for God's action upon and through it. I have stressed that we are embarking upon a way, a journey in the life of faith, and there is no point in disguising that it is an arduous and heroic enterprise. How can it be otherwise? How can the soul be unselfed, its attention systematically transferred from its own interests to God, without effort and a terrible wrestling? Prayer, therefore, must be systematic and it must be arduous. Any athlete will tell you that the time in training that really counts is the time beyond the point of tolerance, the time when you are pushing a little harder than you are really capable of. The same rule applies in prayer. It is true that we must pray as we can and not as we can't, but it is also true that the self's innate tendency is to settle for minimalist prayer, which always gives up at the point of the beginning of discomfort. No growth in prayer is possible without some venture into pain. Baron von Hügel, the most wise and gentle of spiritual guides, explained it like this in a letter to his niece, Gwen.

'... it is perseverance in the spiritual life, on and on, across the years and the changes of our moods and trials, health and environment: it is this that supremely matters. And you will, Gwen, add greatly to the probabilities of such perseverance, if you will get into the way of keeping a little even beyond this time of prayer, when you are dry; and a little short of this time when you are in consolation. You see why, don't you?—Already the Stoics had the grand double rule: "abstain and sustain", i.e. moderate thyself in things attractive and consoling, persevere, hold out, in things repulsive and desolating. There is nothing God loves better, or rewards more richly, than such double self-conquest as this!'

We must banish from our minds all notions that there is an easy and mild and good-natured spirituality, which is all sunshine and shaved lawns and cucumber sandwiches and gentle laughter: that's croquet, not prayer. If you want to be found by God, give yourself arduously to prayer. You are simply wasting your time otherwise, for no dilettante can find the kingdom of God.

Prayer is one type of attention, but the other type of attention is equally important. The only real test of prayer is love. So radical and chronic is the tendency of the self to absorb and utilize everything for its own consumption, that even prayer can become simply an expression or mode of the self's enjoyment of the self. Prayer can become an enjoyable fantasy, unless it has strong moral content, unless it is supported by and leads to love. That, too, can become simply an expression of the ego, another type of self-gratification, another type of self-satisfaction unless it is balanced by and centred in constant self-offering to God. Cheering, isn't it? The self has more twists than a monkey-puzzle. This is not a book about ethics, so I'll say little at this stage about the moral content of prayer, except to remind the reader that prayer which does not issue in love is not prayer, but simply another mode of the self's enjoyment of itself, however subtle. I want, however, to say something in the chapters that follow about the *practice* of prayer.

But there will be no point in going further with this book until the primary decision has been taken. Ask God to show you what *your* Jordan is; what it is that has to be surrendered; where it is that a breach in the fortification of the self must be made; what in you must be humbled and brought low. Then, make the act of surrender, enter your Jordan, wherever you are, and allow God to take your life.

10. PRAYING

The most obvious thing about us is the body. It is the way
way people recognize us and, to a large extent, describe us.
People who love us will be fond of our bodies: the way we
move our hands, or tilt our heads, or throw our hair back out
of our eyes (if there's any left to throw!). A person's body
can be very precious to us: especially when it is no longer
there. The body is the outward and visible sign of the person,
the external part of that sacrament which is personality. I
want to begin thinking about prayer, then, by talking about
the body, because the body is the most basic fact of our
existence and we must come to terms with it if we are to learn
to pray.

One of the most important things to notice about the body
is that it limits us in all sorts of ways. On the most trivial level,
the fact of having a particular body, this body rather than that
body, limits and confines our appearance and physical per-
formance. Our Lord told us that no man by taking thought
can add a span unto his stature: we are stuck with the body
we get, like it or not. This is not a fact which bothers mature
people very much, but it does bother most people when they
are young or if they are immature or seriously disfigured in
some way. We may think that looks do not matter. Health
does. Sometimes the body we are given is deficient: we may
be born with certain predispositions to illness, or some con-
genital disease. Our psychological make-up may be such as to
lead us, later in life, into states of anxiety and depression. It is
true that there is much we can do to overcome the limitations
of the body, but basically we just have to accept it: we are
dealt it at birth and we can't trade it in for a new model, no
matter how limiting or frustrating it may be. That is the first
set of limitations, then: the sheer physical limitations of having
to be what we are given to be.

But the body is more than bone and gristle and hormone.
Our body locates us in a particular background and we can
never escape from it. We are limited genetically: we inherit
characteristics from our parents, whether we like them or not;
we are born into a particular social and historical environment;

and, if certain psychologists are to be believed, our very level of intelligence is decreed at birth. What seems to be beyond dispute is that the first three helpless years of our life are among the most significant that we live. What is done to us then marks and conditions our attitude to life and other people until our life's end, we are told on reliable authority. All of this is packed into us without any reference to our desires or preferences. We are thrown into life, already pro- grammed and limited like some sort of human computer, and we can't alter the basic programme, no matter how much we'd like to.

And the body is with us today. It is the body that defines today what has happened to us, so far, in life. We are still limited by the body today; it still locates us, ties us down to a particular context. It may be, most of the time, for some of us, a sick bed and permanent physical weakness. It may be the quiet onset of old age and all the frustrations of a body which is even more limiting than in the past. It may be that our bodies are trapped where we'd rather not be: a career that no longer satisfies, a life that seems to have lost its promise and purpose. Or it may be that the body today locates us where we're quite contented: a job we enjoy; people we love around us; a life that satisfies. Whatever it is, the body still limits and locates and defines us. It is still the basic fact of our existence: it is the symbol and the sum of all the factors which comprise our life up to this very moment. The body is the symbol, then, the sacrament of what you are. And you can't walk out of it. The body is where you are at this moment.

But the marvellous thing about all this is that you are where God wants you to be: so the body is a sacrament of God's will for you. The body locates you at that point where God is present to you. Let me explain that rather abrupt assertion. According to the teaching of an eighteenth century spiritual director called Jean Pierre de Caussade, whatever our present situation is, it is, in fact, God's will for us and is, therefore, the place appointed for our meeting with him. Accordingly, we are to surrender ourselves to each wave of the sea of life as it comes to us. We are to accept what comes to us because it is God's word to us at that time, even when we hate it. But as well as accepting God's will in the present moment, abandon- ing ourselves to it, we are to cooperate with God in it. The present moment is the only moment in which any kind of action is possible. According to de Caussade, if I want to do the will of God I must recognize that the divine will is always something I must do *now*. I cannot receive now what God will offer me tomorrow, or what he offered me yesterday, but I can receive now what he is offering now. And each moment God is offering me some grace for my acceptance or some command for my obedience. Doing the will of God means receiving the grace and obeying the command moment by moment, now. For this important teaching de Caussade coined the phrase, 'the sacrament of the present moment'. Once you have seen and accepted the validity of this teaching, it has the most liberating effect. You no longer resent your situation or envy that of others; you no longer wish that life had dealt you a different hand, or given you a better start. The life you have is the life which God is using to draw you to himself, and everything that happens to you can be used to draw you nearer to him. Moment by moment you are responding to God's call and God's love: so you start saying 'yes' to life, and you stop saying 'if only'.

This is why the poor old body is so important. The body is the symbol and sacrament of God's will for you at this moment. You are where God would have you be, and where he seeks your cooperation. You are, at this moment, in an appointed place. God wants you to accept your present status and location, no matter how much you loathe it; and he wants you to cooperate with him by finding out what the present situation demands of you. It is not just a matter of passive resignation, of weakly saying 'yes' to superior power. It is acceptance, plus an active cooperation which brings something new, something positive out of the situation. There is no situation, no place in which we find ourselves, where we are not also face to face with God and his will for us. Just as the outward and visible signs of bread and wine convey the real presence of Christ in the Eucharist, so the Sacrament of the Present Moment conveys the real presence of God, if we will accept it and cooperate with it.

I want, therefore, to suggest a method of prayer which affirms this truth and provides a means of union with God through it. I call it the Prayer of the Body, the Prayer of Acceptance. How do we make this kind of prayer?

In any type of prayer, posture is important, especially in the Prayer of the Body. If there is a prayer of the body, then the attitude of the body will be important. The body presents difficulties to prayer. It fidgets, gets stiff, experiences discomfort. These have to be tackled, because they can be symptoms of the distracted and disturbed state of the self. We all know by now the way the body tells the story of the inner life of the self. Apart from the whole range of physical disorders which have their origin in the mind—psychosomatic disorders—there are other obvious signals of the self's dis-ease: tenseness, wringing of the hands, crossing and uncrossing the legs, biting the nails, headaches, heavy smoking and drinking. In all these ways, the self is signalling some distress through the body. Body and mind fuse and interact. In the prayer of the body we can use the body to get at the other aspects of the self, and one of the ways we approach the distracted and disturbed spirit, is by learning to hold an attitude of stillness, simple physical stillness. The attitude we want to develop is one of relaxed alertness. There are two good ways of doing this: one is simply to sit with the back straight, hands on the lap, either held slackly together, or turned palm upwards. Another position for sustained and relaxed prayer is to sit on the heels, or with the legs crossed in front. Kneeling upright, in spite of traditional practice, is not the best way to cultivate the required attitude, though many heroic souls manage to do so. It is not a natural position to relax into, and 'the Anglican crouch' with bottom firmly braced against the pew is mainly conducive to wool-gathering or slumber.

Anyway, this is how we begin: we take up the posture and we relax. An aid to relaxation is deep breathing. Breathe deeply and normally, and observe yourself as you breathe. Concentrate, now, on the simple act of breathing. Put everything else out of your mind. Attend to the body, quietly will any tension away, breathe steadily and rhythmically. Feel the stillness, the simple physical stillness. Attempt nothing else. This is the first phase of the prayer of the body: learning to be still, eyes closed, the whole body relaxed. If you got no further than this every day, you would still be doing something important, because you are doing two things: you are learning to be still and you are learning to concentrate. We should never grudge time spent on the preliminaries to prayer. Most of what humans do in their praying is, simply, to prepare. God gives the prayer. We pay attention. So, hold the body there for a few minutes, concentrate only on that.

After three or four minutes of the simple physical stillness, or as long as it takes to be still, we can go on to the other meaning of what we are doing. As you kneel or sit there, aware of your body which is the sacrament of your very self, accept it. The body is the symbol of you and your history; at this moment in time it represents where you are and what you are, with all the limitations and frustrations of your situation. You are where God wants you to be: accept it. Let your mind lightly gather up in a sort of newsreel what you and your life are at this moment: think of what you resent, what embitters you or frustrates you; think of any whom you are not in love and charity with. Accept it all, say 'yes' to it. Draw it all together, all that your life means and has meant, and focus it all into your body as it kneels or sits, and affirm it: say 'yes' to it all, though tears burn your eyes.

Finally, having affirmed what you are and where you are, and having accepted it, make it available to God. Let your body, symbol of yourself, be abandoned to God, delivered over to him: like a soldier waiting for orders, alert, attentive, unquestioning; or like an exhausted swimmer being brought to land by a life-saver, relaxed and surrendered. Let this phase move into a simple and wordless silence and simply wait there. Do not be in a hurry to get it over with and get on with something important. There is nothing more important. There is only God and you are giving yourself to him.

Then, gradually, come out of the silence. Put your acceptance of God's will and your surrender of yourself to him into a prayer in your own words. And end the prayer time. The Prayer of the Body, then, has three simple phases: stillness; acceptance; surrender.

We have seen how the body defines and represents our limitations, and how we must cultivate an attitude of acceptance to what life brings to it. God comes to us in the sacrament of the present moment. This is a basic truth: God is discovered and disclosed and made present to me in my limitations, in my present condition. Acceptance of the will of God is the very foundation of prayer. But knowledge and union with God is a dynamic thing. It involves not only acceptance, but search and discovery. Christ promised us that the Holy Spirit would guide us into deeper understanding of God; he told us to search in order to find; to go on knocking if we would have the door opened. God, therefore, is not only found in accepting what comes to us – basic though that is – he is found not only in the self and its situation, he is found in the world and in the other person. In other words, there is a prayer of search and discovery, a Prayer of the Mind.

Where do we start this prayer? You can start almost anywhere and it will lead you to God, since he is the source of all things and without him nothing was made that was made. There are lots of books of prayers about this nowadays, all more or less imitations of Abbé Quoist's *Prayers of Life*. Fr Quoist tells us that: 'If we knew how to listen to God, if we knew how to look around us, our whole life would become prayer. For it unfolds under God's eyes and no part of it must be lived without being freely offered to him.' Here is his prayer in *The Underground*.

'The last ones squeeze in.
The door rolls shut.
The train rumbles off.
I can't move.
I am no longer an individual, but a crowd,
A crowd that moves in one piece like jellied soup in its tin.

A nameless and indifferent crowd, probably far from you, Lord.
I am one with the crowd, and I see why it's sometimes hard for me to rise higher.
This crowd is heavy—leaden soles on my feet, my slow feet—a crowd too large for my overburdened skiff.
Yet, Lord, I have no right to overlook these people, they are my brothers,
And I cannot save myself, alone.
Lord, since you wish it, I shall make for heaven in the Underground.'

Many people find that that's how they pray today. They make prayers of life. They meditate upon the meaning of life as it flows around them on the streets, in the underground, on the buses: the tired old lady with her shopping; the children in the swing-park, working themselves higher and higher into the air; a train pulling out of a station and a knot of lonely people waving goodbye. There is plenty of stuff for prayer in any of that. We can come face to face with God through it; we can deepen our knowledge of him.

But Christians have always had a special source of prayer in the Bible, especially in the New Testament. We are people of a book. While all of life is a sacrament of the presence of God, there is a certain ambiguity about it, an uncertainty; God's presence and challenge are blurred and sometimes hazy. In the life of Jesus Christ we see the presence of God with a burning clarity and certainty. To meditate on the New Testament is to discover the inescapable power and presence of God. This may not be immediately self-evident, of course. There are, after all, various ways of using the Bible. Let me list some of them.

There is, first of all, the aesthetic approach, and those who have been reared on the Authorized version are particularly prone to this danger! The Bible becomes an art object to be savoured like a beautiful painting. There is obviously much beauty in the Bible, but this approach can become an escape from the quite personal challenge made to us.

Then there is the historical-development approach. This is the approach found in most places where the Bible is studied. It is summed up in words which Dr Norman Powell Williams applied to the present trend in contemporary theological study: 'At the present time the term "theology" is more commonly used to denote the historical and genetic study of the leading ideas of Christianity, a discipline which does not assume or even investigate the truth of these ideas but is solely interested in discovering the steps of evolutionary process whereby they have come to be what they are.' The Bible is, in its human aspect, the result of a long and complicated process. You can become entangled in that particular bramble bush and never come out again. There is obviously a legitimate place for this particular approach, but it can become obsessive and void the Bible of all challenge.

Related to this approach, but even older, is the use of the Bible as a munitions factory or rock quarry that produces missiles for attack on others. The Bible can be used against people. Out of it are hewn rocks to throw at people. And the Bible can be used as a sweet factory, handing out comforting gobstoppers to suck slowly in moments of tension. That has been one of the ways in which the Bible has helped people, but it can reduce the living and burning Word of God to the status of an anodyne.

All these approaches involve a use of the Bible as though it were a submissive, controllable object which meekly lies to our hand. It is, of course. As was Jesus Christ. But that is not the Christian response. To the Christian, the Bible is not just a beautiful object; or a fascinating problem; or a useful source of ammunition against one's theological opponents; or a comfort factory. In all these ways of using the Bible, *we* are in control: we admire, or interrogate, or chuck it or suck it, while it is passive. But the Bible is the Word of God. It is God come in search of us. What would be your response if, without any shadow of doubt, you knew that God was addressing you? Would it not be the response of T. S. Eliot to *Little Gidding*?

'You are not here to verify,
Instruct yourself or inform curiosity
Or carry report. You are here to kneel.'

The Bible is God's word addressed quite personally to us, and the only way to know the truth of that statement is to start using the Bible as though it were true. To approach it humbly and expectantly. To read it on your knees, as someone put it. To come to it as to a word from God addressed with absolute appropriateness to yourself. No amount of argument can establish the claim I have just made. It can only be established by experience. The Bible is like Jesus Christ. It is possible to avoid the quite personal challenge he makes to us by putting up a diversionary smokescreen of difficulties.

There are two ways in which the Bible can become the word of God for us, and the first feeds the second. This is the systematic, liturgical use of Scripture. Read daily over the years it becomes part of one. It becomes an environment in which we move. There are many lectionaries, missals, prayer books, office books, systems, which are based on this method of continuous reading.

The second way of reading the Bible is called meditation, and it is best done with a pen in your hand and a notebook in front of you. It involves allowing a passage of scripture to open up to us something of God. The same method can be used on a favourite hymn or poem. Method is important in this type of prayer, but it should never be followed slavishly. Method is a springboard to get us going, not something we do for its own sake. And the most important part of the method is choosing the passage to pray about! Don't leave it to chance, and don't go through the Bible with a safety pin. Plan your prayer. The simplest method is to use the daily readings provided by the various lectionaries, or to spin out during the following week the scripture passages used at the Eucharist on the previous Sunday. However you do it, do not leave it till the minute before you are going to pray. Know in advance what your passage is going to be, then go apart to pray.

Here's what I do, and there are a hundred and one variations on this particular method. Your bible is open at the correct place, and you have a notebook and pencil beside you. Now, just because we are attempting a different phase of prayer, there is no point in forgetting the first thing we learnt: the prayer of the body is foundational. Always begin in this way: take up the prayer attitude and pray and breathe your way into stillness. When you are still, say a short prayer in your own words or from a book, asking for the guidance of the Holy Spirit. Then read the passage over slowly, which you have chosen. Savour it. If anything immediately catches your attention, stay with it; never rush on. Method, remember, is something to get you going, not something to hold you back. Having read over the passage, go through the following phases:

Pick out and write down all the people in the scene.

Describe it all: note how each person acts and speaks and stands in relation to the central figure, Jesus. (This is not an invariable pattern. If you are meditating on a saying of our Lord you would omit both the first phases and move straight to phase three.)

In phase three you write down the answer to the following questions:

What does this passage tell me about Jesus and about God? God before my eyes.

What does this story tell me about myself? God in my heart.

What does this story tell me about the will of God for my life? God in my hands.

Finally, turn what you have learned into a short and very earnest prayer, asking God to help you to carry it into your daily life.

*   *   *

So far, we have thought about prayer as acceptance and discovery. In the Prayer of the Body we accept, say 'yes' to God's will for us as we are, with all the limitations and possibilities of our state. This is the foundation of prayer. We have to affirm and accept our situation as the basis for everything else that we do.

The Prayer of the Mind is a more active type of prayer. It is based on the belief that the character of God and his continuing will for us can be discovered by a process of reflection. By a process of holy thinking in the presence of Scripture, we can discover more about God and his will for us.

Now, both these types of prayer have two things in common. They tend to presuppose a separation between ourselves and God. In the first case, God has put us into a particular situation and we have to get on with life in it. But the getting on with it assumes a certain distance from God, a certain independent responsibility on my part. This is even clearer in the Prayer of the Mind. God's will and character are out there, in the Bible for instance, and we work away at uncovering them, unravelling the code which conceals his message to us. So both these types of prayer presuppose a certain distance between ourselves and God. More importantly, each of these methods of prayer tends to focus activity in the self. In the Prayer of the Body it is *my* situation I affirm and accept. In the prayer of the Mind it is *my* thought which discovers God's will for and message to *me*.

To a very great extent, this is all true enough. We are at a distance from God, or so it seems often enough; and the self is the main reality in our life. We cannot unself ourselves any more than we can climb out of our own skins. Everything seems unavoidably located in the self. This, in fact, is our main problem. If we are honest, we'll admit that most of the time God is not real for us. He does not have the unavoidable reality that other people have or that our own mind has. This conviction has a subtle influence on our prayer. Since we don't really believe that God is *there,* our prayer becomes busy and humanistic. The Prayer of the Body can become the power of positive thinking, a cunning way of talking ourselves into accepting situations we can't or don't know how to, change. And the Prayer of the Mind can become a little sermon we make up and preach to ourselves. We goad ourselves on to behave better, by entertaining thoughts about our Lord in our mind. All the time, we are not sure whether God is speaking to us through all this, or whether we are just speaking, speaking, speaking to ourselves. Because we are not really sure there is anything out there to hear us, our prayer 'Is cries countless, cries like dead letters to dearest him that lives, alas! away!', in Hopkin's words.

A moment's reflection should convince us of the folly of this attitude. How can God be at a distance from us? Where can he be if he is somewhere else? God fills all things and surrounds all things. St Augustine said that God was a circle whose centre is everywhere and whose circumference is nowhere. There *is* nowhere where God is not. And the reality of

God is the only really real thing there is! Every other reality has been called into existence by him. They exist by his will. There is something ironic about the way God's creatures fret and fuss about his existence. They would have no power to fret and fuss about his reality if it were not given them by him whom they doubt! It is as though the pot questioned the reality of the hands of the potter who spun it on the wheel. The fact is that some strange paralysis, some strange blindness afflicts us: we are like blind men in a many-coloured universe who argue that all is grey.

God is within us. We don't need to go on elaborate explorations of external reality to discover traces of his presence, like detectives hunting for clues. He is within us, closer to us than our own breathing. There is a third type of prayer which is a celebration of this fact, above all other facts.

In the Prayer of the Heart we travel inwards to gaze upon God and be with him. This type of prayer is sometimes called contemplation and people think of it as being the most difficult type of prayer there is, suitable only for budding mystics and fully-fledged saints. Part of the awe in which it is held is caused by the fact that it is not easy to describe; it can only be done, like swimming or cycling. Since it is a wordless type of prayer, it is almost impossible to describe in words either how to do it or what happens during it. Another difficulty in this type of prayer is that it involves the loss of self-awareness and it bypasses the mind: how can we describe to ourselves the losing of the sense of ourselves. How can the mind explain a state that is not a state of mind? Though it is difficult to describe, there are related experiences which we all have which are easier to identify, and we can use these as analogies.

There are many things in life which draw out a response from us which we cannot put into words or even entirely understand. The experience of beauty is the most common example. When we come across something of great beauty it can have a strange effect upon us. We do not, at the time, analyse it or try to account for its power. It draws us out of ourselves, it 'sends us'. It can be a piece of music; a sudden and heart-breaking glimpse of a lovely valley through a break in the clouds from high on a hill; or a thrill of love and tenderness at the sight of a face we care deeply for: a child asleep, or the unselfconscious gesture which entirely captures the endearing particularity of someone we love. Or it can be that strange and marvellous experience in reading a book or listening to someone speak, when we recognize something as being right and true, though not with our minds, rather with our whole being, with a surge of recognition from the very depths of the self.

These experiences have two things in common: They draw us out from ourselves; we lose awareness of ourselves and become, as it were, eyes gazing upon something beyond the self. This is almost the purest joy that life affords. And surely that is significant. All our happiest and most exalted moments are moments of unselfconsciousness. The reason for this is obvious. We were never meant to enjoy *ourselves* in the first place! Real joy, real happiness is ec-static—it stands out from the self in the other. This kind of real joy can be the main characteristic of a life we might judge to be most miserable. It is the joy of the martyrs, the joy of the crucified, who have ceased to exist for themselves at all. This teaches us that real joy is never self-conscious, never an enjoying of the self: it is always an enjoyment of something beyond the self. Secondly, none of these experiences provides us with lasting satisfaction or happiness. They are fleeting. They raise us for a moment. They take us out of ourselves for an instant, and then leave us forlorn. They are promises which never, quite, fulfil themselves. The reason for this, too, is obvious. These things which draw us out of ourselves, like ourselves, have no reality in themselves at all. They are reflections of God, echoes of his footsteps. They pierce us with longing, but they cannot fulfil us, because they are not ultimately real in themselves. They are *created* and we long for and can only be satisfied by the *uncreated*. Only God will do.

In the Prayer of the Heart, we enjoy him who lies behind all the promise and all the longing of creation: we enjoy God and for himself alone. Nothing comes between him and us: no self-concern, not even penitence; no thinking about God, for that always centres the activity in my mind; no speaking to God, for that is to use my voice and my words. In the Prayer of the Heart we become ears that simply take in the music; eyes that gaze upon the scene; the good earth that receives both rain and sunshine. We become an empty cup for God to fill. How do we do it?

Well, the question puts us in the wrong place straight away, because we don't really do anything. That is what is so difficult: learning *not* to do, not to think, not to make pictures in our mind, not to worry or plan or get restless. We are, simply,

to *be*: like the earth beneath the sun, or the hearth on which
the fire burns. Of course, we'll begin by trying to be as still
as we can, in the way in which I have described. It helps, too,
to repeat a phrase from the psalms or some other part of
scripture over and over, rhythmically, to keep the mind occu-
pied gently, while the stillness builds underneath. If we make
use of this kind of repetition, it is important to remember that
we are not to *think* about what we are saying. Its use is rather
like the use of beads, as a means of concentrating and stilling
the mind. What happens is not to be expressed in prose. Instead, let me express it in a prayer I found somewhere.

> 'Serene light shining in the ground of my being, draw me to
>   yourself.
> Draw me past the snares of the senses, out of the mazes of
>   the mind.
> Free me from symbols, from words,
> That I may discover the signified, the word unspoken,
> In the darkness that veils the ground of my being. Amen.'

So far, I have not said a word about what most people mean
by prayer: asking God for something. At some time in their
lives most people have done this. They may not be religious;
they may never think of God at all in normal circumstances,
but in an emergency they find themselves praying desperately:
'Don't let him die, God!' 'End the war!' 'Stop the plague!'
'Send rain!' This is the most common type of prayer: the cry
for help. It has its origin in the sense of helplessness the person
feels. There is nothing humanly left to do, nothing in the world
to turn to, so he turns, at last, to God. This turning to God as
a last resort is not prayer, though it can be the beginning of
prayer. If it brings the person to an awareness of his own in-
completeness and futility, it can be the beginning of real
prayer. In most cases, this does not happen. Most people don't
take it any further. Nothing happens. They never bother to
examine the meaning of the strange thing they did, that
mysterious cry of help that was wrenched out of them.

Now, the first thing we learn from this strange impulse in
man to scream for help in time of trouble, is that this life, this
world, is not ultimately dependable. We can't really put our
trust in it. Sooner or later, if we do, the feet will be wiped out
from under us. There is no firm foundation, nothing that gives
lasting security in this life. Sooner or later we all find this out,

even if it takes the old enemy, death, to do it. At this point man finds nothing in the world in which to trust, nothing to turn to, and he finds this strange instinct within him which says 'turn to God'. But he does not really turn to *God*. He wants to hold on to the world and he calls to God to help him do that. 'Make the world secure', he says to God, 'make it trustworthy and unchanging.' Do you see what he is doing? He is asking for the *world* to be made God. He is at the point where he might, at last, recognize that only God is dependable and unchanging and trustworthy: God offers him himself, but he says, 'Not you, not you. Give me back the world. Give me another five minutes'. His prayer never quite becomes prayer, because he's trying to use God to get his own way.

But let's suppose that he sees the truth. He accepts the knowledge that the fashion of this world changes and decays and only God is sure. He begins to pray. Prayer is that activity by which we grow in union with God. In true prayer, the awareness of the self is lost, if only for a moment, and God becomes all in all. We ask nothing for ourselves, for he who possesses God and is possessed by him needs nothing else. It takes less than a moment to realize that we have not reached that stage of complete absorption in God, in which his will is our will. We are still well aware of our little selves, conscious of our needs and desires. They are still very much part of us. Very well, these, too, must be brought to God. Prayer of this sort is called 'Petition', and it is nothing to be ashamed of. Our Lord included it in his pattern prayer when he told us to ask for our daily bread; and he told his disciples to ask and they would receive. How do we pray in this way?

Our purpose in prayer is to increase our abandonment to God, the surrender of the self. Part of the self is that bundle of needs and desires, some half-formed, some fully articulated; some we are half-ashamed of, some we desperately long for. Don't be ashamed of any of them. They are part of you and they have to be given to God. Offer them to God as they are. Not, however, in a spirit of craving or defiance; rather, in a spirit of acceptance, possibly of humour. 'Here I am Lord, a weird bundle of longings and desires, of ambitions and fears. Take me and them and do with them according to thy will. I'd like to pass that examination, or get that new job, or find some joy in my life. I'd like to be really well again, or less irritable and more loving. I'm not really brave enough to pretend that I'm not bothered about what happens to me.

Nevertheless, thy will be done, because I know that, in the long run, thy will is my happiness.' The important thing in the prayer of petition is, first of all, to be what you are without trying to cover up; and, secondly, to let God deal with your needs in his way, knowing that his way is your peace.

Praying for ourselves is called Petition, though it often shades into praying for others, which we call Intercession. Intercession is really one aspect of love in action. If God is the source of all joy and happiness, then we'll want to bring to him those whom we love and those for whom we care, and this includes the dead as well as the living. I have never been able to understand the kind of mind that denounces prayer for the dead as some kind of unmentionable perversion. Just because people are dead is no reason to stop loving them. My mother died two years ago. I still love her and think about her and pray for her. Nothing could be more natural. The fact that biological or somatic death has intruded upon our relationship is no reason for me to end my care and concern for her. We do not know the exact state of the dead, but for Christians' to die is Christ', so my prayer for the dead is a prayer in Christ. And there is another consideration. The Christian Church is not just the aggregate of all living Christians: it is the total of all those who have ever been Christians. The old division used to be, The Church Triumphant in Heaven, Expectant in Paradise, Militant here on earth. To confine one's care or concern or interest simply to those who are alive, is a peculiar foreshortening of the imagination and a narrowing of the heart. I feel very close indeed to a number of Christians, long dead, whose teaching helps me still. One's dead loved ones as well as all the living, are all part of that self which we are daily surrendering to God; they are in the heart we offer daily to God. Intercession is the explicit and self-conscious gathering together of those whom we love and have a responsibility for, into our self-offering to God. Again, we must remember the two rules: to be ourselves, and to let God deal with it in his own way. We never come to God or to anyone else, alone. We are always tied to, and associated with many others. We intercede for them by consciously bringing them with us into the heart of God.

But intercession is more momentous, even, than that. God has given us the power and the freedom to make a difference in the world. We are used to this idea in the realm of the natural universe. Our actions make a difference, for good or ill, in the natural universe. But they also make a difference in the world of spirit, in the supernatural world. For obvious reasons, of course, the difference is often disguised from us. We can never know the exact effect of our prayers in the way we can know the effect of our physical action, but they do make a difference. This is why it is true to say that, in the long run, all prayer is answered. In Christian prayer we always pray according to his will; we seek to cooperate with God's work of restoring creation to its original joy in him. We cannot tell the battles that are waged between God and the mystery of evil which seeks constantly to frustrate his will, but we do know that in the end all will be well. Intercession, meanwhile, is one of the weapons for our part of the battle of God's love with the power of evil. Our prayers are weapons of spirit in this great conflict, but they are under the command of God who alone knows how to dispose them effectively.

If it is asked why God cannot bring all this to pass without our assistance, then the short answer is that, doubtless, he could if he wanted to, but he has chosen to give us a role. He has made us free. It could be argued that he could easily organize things in a way that would not involve us in any free act at all. But he has made us free spirits, not little robots. He allows us to make a difference, because he wants us to co-operate with him in his work of love. Something else follows from this. We lose power if we don't use it. This is obvious in the physical realm. If we never walk we soon lose the power of our legs. This is just as true in the spiritual order. We can allow our spiritual powers to atrophy, to lose their effectiveness. This is particularly true of the power of prayer. We cannot tell what impact upon time and the world is made by the prayers of God's children, but we can be quite sure it makes an enormous difference, a difference that runs through time and into eternity. If we want to be powerful intercessors, then we must exercise the intercessory power we have, frequently and systematically. There really is as little point in asking someone to pray for you if they rarely pray, as there is in asking someone who has spent the last five years in bed to join you in climbing Ben Nevis.

Most of those who take this work seriously keep a little notebook in which they keep the names of those for whom they pray. A fascinating part of such systematic intercession is to note how frequently, even in this life, our prayers are answered. It is a tremendous power we are given. It seems a pity not to use it.

'O Holy Spirit, giver of light and life,
Impart to us thoughts higher than our own thoughts,
And prayers better than our own prayers,
And powers beyond our own powers;
That we may spend and be spent in the ways of love and
   goodness. Amen.'

11. BLESSING

In chapter two I suggested the fourfold pattern of the eucharistic action as the way in which we come to God, or the way to the place where God comes to us. I said that we had to be taken, consecrated, broken and distributed, as Christ was, and as the Holy Bread in the eucharist is. By prayer we surrender ourselves to God, we offer ourselves that he might take us. I have spent some time talking about prayer, about this activity of surrender, because I am increasingly aware that all sorts of people want quite specific guidance in prayer, they want to know what they must 'do'. What I have suggested is practical, however superficial. I'm sure that there is no progress in the knowledge of God that is not by prayer, and we must start somewhere. I have suggested one or two starting points. The temptation that confronts anyone who is interested in the spiritual life is to make himself into something of a theoretical expert on prayer, while spending very little time on the exercise itself. Every priest has what George MacLeod calls a bankrupt corner in his library, filled with dozens of little books and large, on the life of prayer, testimony to the time given to the study of the subject. But every priest has a bankrupt corner in his heart, where he knows that he has failed in the practice of praying: he may be able to enumerate the steps in an Ignation meditation, but it is probably a long time since he made one. There is only one thing to do in a situation like that, and that is to start again! And it does not require elaborate equipment or lengthy preparation. It only takes a little time, to begin with. In time, by God's grace, it will take a long time. In most lives, praying is something we start over and over again. Well, that does not matter either. It is something, after all, to go on struggling. I want, now, to look at the second phase in the fourfold pattern of sacrifice, the phase of anointing or consecration.

God's immediate response to our offering of ourselves in prayer is to pour out upon us a special blessing. He takes, and then he blesses our life. He endows us with his own spirit, his own grace. Again, we are not talking about a once-and-for-all event, in which God gives us an inoculation of grace which lasts till death. I have already pointed out that the will is not a static object which we can simply hand over to God once and for all. The will is dynamic and giving it to God is a constant process, constantly repeated. And Grace exactly corresponds to this character. God's Grace or Spirit is not a sort of plastic substance which is inserted into the soul and acts henceforth upon it like a homing device in a glider. God's grace is dynamic and personal, it is God himself loving us and willing us on, cheering and supporting us. Like the will which we constantly give over to God, God's Grace is constantly poured out upon us in exact correspondence to our activity of self-surrender. Perhaps an illustration will help here.

Everywhere that the President of the USA. goes he is accompanied by a quiet and unobtrusive member of the armed forces, who carries a little black box. If the need arose, the President could send out an immediate order, through the little box, to place the American Air Force on nuclear alert. Within seconds, the whole arsenal of American nuclear might could be winging its way to its chosen target. Beyond a certain point, the Failsafe point, they could not be withdrawn. In the early days of the Cold War, before we learnt to live with the knowledge that we are poised permanently on the edge of nuclear disaster, this situation of nuclear readiness gave rise to a spate of novels and films, all designed to exploit the precariousness of our situation. We have, as I said, learnt to live with the knowledge, by pushing it out of consciousness. Meanwhile, we live out our average day beneath the volcano. The irony is that this situation of preparedness, of instant, synchronized reaction to threat, is a ghastly parody of the Grace and Mercy of God. There is a divine synchronicity, an attitude of permanent alertness in Heaven which enables Grace to respond instantly to man's call and need. It is shown with particular effectiveness in Edwin Muir's poem, *The Good Man in Hell*. In the poem, Muir meditates on the possibility of a good man finding himself in Hell, 'by needful error of the qualities' and, by his very faithfulness, undoing Hell.

> 'Would he at last, grown faithful in his station,
>   Kindle a little hope in hopeless Hell,
> And sow among the damned doubts of damnation,
> Since here someone could live and could live well?

One doubt of evil would bring down such a grace,
Open such a gate, all Eden could enter in,
Hell be a place like any other place,
And love and hate and life and death begin.'

The Grace of God is poised over us, ready to penetrate and forgive at the very instant our need expresses itself: 'Betwixt the stirrup and the ground, Mercy I asked, mercy I found.' This was the knowledge which Christ laboured to make known: the infinite and unremitting accessibility of Grace. The Prodigal son is met by his father while he is a great way off. The penitent thief is promised eternal life on the basis of a single, honest and kindly insight. The mercies of God hover over us in a state of permanent alert. This knowledge has led to a calculating cynicism or libertarianism on the part of some, with a carefully postponed repentance till the last possible moment, a technique greatly favoured by certain Roman Emperors. We can be quite sure that even here God finds a sufficient germ of repentance to work on. God's grace responds instantly to every tremor of longing that we feel. He wants to take us so that he can consecrate us.

The action of God in consecrating us is twofold. Consecrating or blessing is, in one of its aspects, a process of setting-apart, of dedicating to a special, an exclusive use and purpose. There is something frightening about this. The creature is set aside, has allowed itself to be set aside, for divine service. Of course, it goes without saying, that divine service is as wide as the life and work of mankind. What happens is that the self makes itself entirely available for God's use and henceforth God's will is the motive power of all its activity. It is the *attitude* of the will that is important. Having given yourself to God, you are no longer your own. You have no disposable assets which are yours to play with. You are God's own possession, stamped with his seal. From now on you are holy in the original meaning of the word: you are set apart for God's use. And God ratifies that self-offering by receiving and blessing and affirming it.

'God has put his seal upon us and given us his Spirit in our hearts as a guarantee.' 2 Cor.2.22.

The thought must immediately enter itself: 'What about falling-away? What if one makes the gift, the offering of oneself, and it is received and ratified, stamped with the seal of the Spirit, and then we steal it back again?' Our Lord himself uttered some terrible words about this: 'No one who puts his hand to the plough and looks back is fit for the kingdom of God'. Luke 9.62. And I'm not talking about 'sinning'. There is a remedy and medicine for that in the Sacrament of Reconciliation. I'm talking about the gift of the will to God and its fraudulent return to the self. Individual moments of weakness and failure will come. We can expect them and need not regard them too highly. What is more important is that gradual fastening of the will back onto the self so that the new life is either abandoned altogether or observed only by a few token observances; or the new life simply becomes yet another vehicle for the pathology of the self. Religion becomes an expression of our selfishness. It becomes a means of parading our self-importance, or a support for our prejudices, or a warm blanket to keep out the draughts that blow in from the world. That's what is likely to happen to people who are attached to religion for the wrong reasons. Those who are not interested in religion as a human activity, are more likely to revert to previous patterns of sporadic and desultory activity. All this is possible and we know it, but so does the Grace of God, which rises to meet the dangers at every point. And this brings me to the second aspect of this sanctifying and consecrating action of God: the gift of the Spirit.

So far, almost everything I've said has been rather bleak and chilling. There is a kind of religion which never gets beyond this emphasis. Sometimes the atmosphere in a certain kind of religious house suggests what I'm talking about: a grim and echoing barrenness; heels, staccato on polished tiles; the noise of a door shutting somewhere back in the building; and an absence of something, an absence of spring and summer and heart-breaking autumn—a permanent winter of the heart, like Narnia, the land where it is always December but never Christmas. And some people give off the same atmosphere: lips pulled down at the corners, sullenly battling against the mystery of iniquity. All this is a Christianity which appears to have been offered and taken, but never blessed, never anointed with the oil of gladness. It is a religion of the wilderness without knowledge of the Resurrection. And most of us have that kind of idea of religion fixed firmly within us. We have an idea that religion is all about giving up, and is not mainly about receiving; it's about a God who demands sacrifices that make our hearts wince, but who never offers anything in return.

This is one reason we are so hesitant and slow to bring our-selves to God: because we don't really like him. If we believe in him at all, he is a sort of formal principle: the symbol of all the laws and rules instilled by parents and society. He is the super-ego, that part of ourselves, buried deep within, which disapproves of so much and especially of those untamed and often unnamed desires. A religion of bleak landscapes and dark, gothic buildings and barred windows and gusting winds and the old sinking anxiety of being lost. In short, a religion without Gospel; it is a religion of the cross without the resur-rection; a religion of surrender and not a religion of victory. And the Christian Faith, if only we would see it, is a religion of victory, a religion of enabling power, of grace, of blessing. All those acts of denial and self-surrender are but the neces-sary concomitants of the reception of God's amazing gift of grace. Like the beggar in all those fairy stories which are about you and me, we must strip off our rags (and possibly take a bath) only because we are being clothed upon with the gar-ments of joy and gladness. We are offered the very Spirit of God as our anointing. We are to take up a heroic vocation, to be sure, but we are also offered the power to fulfil it. We are offered for our lives the very power, in Paul's words, which raised Christ from the dead, the power of God. This power exactly corresponds to the challenges that await us. The chal-lenge of temptation to sin is matched by the grace to overcome the temptation; the challenge to witness for God is matched by the power of God within us, giving us, if necessary, the very words we need. Every challenge that the suffering and confusion of the world places before us draws from us, by the power of the Spirit, an appropriate response. Yet the para-dox holds: God does not switch us on to a sort of automatic pilot which he then controls. We are still in control, our will must be given over to God moment by moment, and his grace corresponds to that activity; nay, his grace *prompts* our activity of self-offering, so that we can feel the full power of Paul's classic paradox which states the central psychological experience of the Christian life: 'I live; yet no longer I; Christ liveth in me.'

There are parts of the Christian Church today, and many individual Christians, that have lost all expectation that God might do any new work in the world through them, that any witness might be borne to his Gospel. Their religion has be-come formal, intellectual, institutional. There is little sense in them that God can actually do anything anymore, certainly no sense that he can do anything through them! Part of the problem lies in a wrong estimate of Christ, as well as a low estimate of themselves. Christ is thought by many to be *unlike* them in all things, including sin. They reverse the insight of the Letter to the Hebrews that Christ was like us in all things, except sin. At the back of many minds is the Docetic Christ, the Christ who was really a phantom. For him miracles and heroism and the ability to bring men and women to God came easily, because he was God incarnate. He was disguised as a poor, fallible human being, like us, but inside he was all divine power. Like Superman who appears to be a mild, bespectacled young man but who has this tremendous secret power, so it is with Christ. He only has to nip into the broom cupboard to get into his gear, and then he's off on a dazzling display of supernatural overkill. After all, after his baptism we read:

'And when Jesus was baptized, he went up immediately from the water, and behold the heavens were opened and he saw the Spirit of God descending like a dove, and alighting on him; and lo, a voice from heaven, saying, "This is my beloved Son, with whom I am well pleased."'   Matt. 3.16–17.

The reason why the Christian Church has been so careful in its statement of the meaning and nature of Christ is because of its entirely proper conviction that wrong belief always leads to confusion in the Christian life. The concern over heresy is a concern, not for doctrinal exactitude, but for practical discipleship. Nowhere is this more true than in the doctrine of the Incarnation. Christians maintain the paradox that Christ was man, fully man and truly man. He was totally identified with us. He achieved what he achieved, not because he was God dressed up as man, but because he was a man completely surrendered to God. It was the *humanity* of Christ that worked wonders, a humanity empowered by God, because it had been surrendered to God. And we are offered the same arrangement! Our Lord himself told us that if we would believe in him, put our trust in him without compromise and qualification, we would do the works that he did, and greater works than these. We find these words in John's Gospel, the Gospel where the mystery of the Incarnation is expressed with quite explicit clarity. John will not let us fudge or elude the nature of Christ as God and man. In his manhood God was fully at work, because his manhood had been offered and consecrated by the power of God.

'Truly, truly, I say to you, he who believes in me will also do the works that I do; and greater works than these will he do, because I go to the Father. Whatever you ask in my name, I will do it, that the Father may be glorified in the Son; if you ask anything in my name, I will do it'.   John 14.12-14.

Christians have proved the truth of this dramatic promise in their own experience. His disciples, down the ages, have done greater works than he ever did: they have converted millions, healed countless diseases, brought wholeness to generations of the broken, enriched the whole of human culture; but only because they allowed the full and majestic power of God to work through them. St Augustine put it like this: 'Without God we cannot; without us God will not.' We are offered this, yet we hold back! We are offered this work of being a partner with God in the healing and restoration of his creation, and we settle—for what? What have you settled for? What is your private alternative to the only true human vocation? What banality have you preferred to the sublimity that is laid before you? What form does your idol take? Search yourself. Admit your cowardice. Then offer yourself, knowing that God will immediately respond with grace to sustain your commitment, and receive his Spirit for the struggle that lies ahead. Allow yourself to be taken, and suffer yourself to be blessed!

12. BREAKING

Many stories and films, for adults as well as children, end with
a satisfying climax in which all difficulties are resolved, justice
is done, true love wins its way, and all live happily ever after.
The ingredients may vary of course. It may be a story of
romantic love. After many misunderstandings and misadven-
tures and narrow escapes, the hero rides off into the sunset with
the heroine sitting behind him to keep a date with the preacher
in Dodge City. Or it may be a story of spiritual love and dedication, and we leave the hero or heroine, having made the
great act of renunciation, kneeling before the altar to commit
themselves to the heavenly marriage. The orchestra swells
and the cameras soar above the lonely, kneeling figure, the
symbol of commitment after struggle, of peace after strife,
the symbol of Hopkin's *Nun Taking the Veil:*

'I have desired to go
Where springs not fail,
To fields where flies no sharp and sided hail
And a few lilies blow.

And I have asked to be
Where no storms come,
Where the green swell is in the havens dumb,
And out of the swing of the sea.'

Artistically and dramatically it is all very satisfying. It finishes
the story with an entirely appropriate climax. The lights go up
and we dab our eyes and gather up our coats; or we lay the
book down, the last page completed, with a satisfied sadness.
It is all neat and tidy, with no loose ends. All brought to a
fitting conclusion. And all terribly unreal, and in a fundamental way, dishonest. Because we all know the story is far from
over. We know that before they get to Dodge City they'll have
fallen out, because the saddle's hurting her bottom and he
didn't help her down when they stopped at that water hole at
Coyote Gulch. The real story, in fact, is just starting, and along
the marriage trail they'll encounter more danger and mishap
than anything Geronimo threw at them. And the same is true

of spiritual marriage. The dedicated young novices will soon find that the struggle is only just beginning as the convent door closes behind them and the relatives all go home.

In fact, there are no fitting and dramatic climaxes in our lives which resolve all our difficulties and issue in a new age without tears and struggle. And that may be why we have this appetite for unreality and escape in our stories and plays. We like to escape into the fairy tale. That's fine, as long as it is kept within bounds. But it isn't. In a very real way we try to make life imitate art, instead of allowing art to mirror life. As a result we're permanently dissatisfied. The reality never does fit the dream we had: the romance soon wears off, and it's business as usual, with a longing look over the shoulder at the fantasy that started it all. We try to base our lives on romantic fiction. This is true on all the important levels of life. It accounts for the unreality in many marriages, based, as they often are, on a set of expectant fantasies, rather than on the hard knowledge that living together, though ultimately rewarding, is a costly and demanding process. And the same goes for any community. There are no heavenly choruses: only a permanent battle against irritation and ill-adjusted relationships.

The fantasy life we prefer is very prevalent in our religious expectations. Having, in a moment of heroic dedication or a fit of absentmindedness, abandoned our life to the Lord to be taken and consecrated and used, we think that ought to be that. The trumpets have sounded and our hearts, maybe, have been strangely warmed, and that, according to the convention, ought to be the end. In fact, it is only the beginning and the real struggle is only about to begin.

You see, we are still engaged in that taxing process of unwinding the self from that tight defensive and self-sufficient ball into an open and, therefore, unprotected and unguarded response to God and others. We are now placed where we can learn to love, really to love, in a costing way. But we can't love all in a flash. We can't transform our attitude into one of permanent warmth and acceptance, like a sort of practised smile. This love, this living out of the reality of love, is a series of endless adjustments and responses, it is an active process, not a static endowment. Part of that response is negative and painful, because the process of unwinding the self, of prising it open, is a kind of death. God has to break us up in order to make us available for distribution. We have been taken and consecrated, set apart and empowered for a life of service and devotion. Now it starts. Everyone has gone home. The stimulus and drama of the audience has been withdrawn. Now we must enter the desert of lonely struggle. The battle for the self really begins. And most of us resist our own death. We do not want to be broken.

What is it in you that has to break up and die, before God's power can really take hold and work? Almost certainly, there is sin: some habit, some activity of self-regard that feeds itself by starving others; it may be a particular sin or weakness, something we cling to with destructive frenzy. It may be more diffuse: a general style of living that is cosily and privately selfish. There may be no major area of dramatic weakness, but there is a routine and attitude which is carefully arranged to seal us off from too much outside pressure and interference. We are all very good at erecting protective fortifications and escaping behind them as often as possible. Well, the Lord is going to have to blow up all our Berlin walls and tear down our drawbridges; unless, of course, we want to bury ourselves in there and live entirely on ourselves and for ourselves. When the last trump sounds to summon us all to reality, how many of us will crawl out of these little citadels, blinded by the light we were meant to live by?

Or it may be our own reserve and fastidiousness that has to be broken up. We want to preserve our cool, retain our composure. We don't want to stand out, or behave oddly. Even if we venture out from behind the castle walls, we'll look straight ahead and keep a firm grip on our umbrella. The Lord may have to break through all that. He may have to thaw out all those good manners we've hidden behind for years, and force a strange laughter from that stiff, upper lip. We must be broken up. The ice must break before the river can flow again.

Or maybe it is our mind: the little god reason or intellect which many of us have inside, barking and sneering at every sudden access of feeling, scoffing and doubting every emotion. The mind, too, has to be surrendered, broken up, but not in the name of irrationality, but because we make a god and king out of it. In all these ways, we are doing homage to the self, and we've got to be broken from them all before we can be really free. Any addict is a slave, living in a terrible misery and bondage. To achieve freedom he has to go through a terrible process of withdrawal, a real dying, a real breaking-up. He has to go though an awful, howling wilderness, before coming to the promised land of freedom. There's no way of avoiding the process. There are no shortcuts that go round the wilderness. You have to go through it. And the addict is only a particularly heightened illustration of everyman's status, a sort of hideous cartoon of the human condition. We are all fixated on the self, and the price of freedom is that costly process of dying, of being broken up. There's no other way. We must be taken and consecrated and *broken*.

If we think we can avoid this, remember the story of Christ, our pattern and our way. Christ did not go from his baptism, from the moment of consecration and endowment, to a reception which congratulated him on the gift of the Spirit. He went into the desert to wrestle and be broken. Mark tells the story briefly. After the baptism of Jesus, we read:

'The Spirit immediately drove him out into the wilderness. And he was in the wilderness forty days, tempted by Satan; and he was with the wild beasts; and the angels ministered unto him.'   Mark 1.12–13

The story of the temptations of Christ is one of the best known stories in the Gospels. The first temptation was to change stones into bread, to satisfy an urgent and immediate physical need which was tyrannous in its insistence. In a sense it is true to say that the first temptation is the most basic and universal of all temptations. As creatures, we are a turbulent mixture of needs and desires. Our physical nature is enormously powerful. Programmed into us, in our battle for survival as a species, is a whole range of drives and needs: the sexual drive, the need to feed ourselves, the need to find shelter and to make it safe and comfortable. These needs are part of our nature. They are God-given. They are good. But because there is a strange imbalance in our nature, a flaw, a fault, these neutral and necessary drives become strangely distorted and take on a dynamism of their own; they assume a role that is far beyond their proper status. They become totalitarian, and threaten to take over our whole nature, leaving the more sensitive parts of our make-up exposed and vulnerable to their brute power. The need for shelter, for instance, becomes an obsessive craving for possessing more and more and more, a dynamically ascending lust for comfort and affluence. Where it has the means to satisfy itself, this drive can lead to the ostentatious life-style of the super affluent with their vast palaces, carefully guarded, set in acres of parkland, protected from trespass and violation by others. In time, this positive drive for the ultimate shelter becomes a negative fear of those who might threaten it, and a whole theory is developed to justify having more than all the others. None of us is protected from this crushing urge. We may not be millionaires, but compared to the desert dwellers of the Sahel or the occupants of shanty towns in Rio de Janeiro, we occupy the same role. The Western phenomenon of constantly upgrading the standard of living, of pushing up and up towards the ultimate in creature-comfort, is a manifestation of this need. It is the need for shelter become pathological. Since we live in a finite world with limited resources, this ascending scale of comfort can only be maintained at the expense of others, in our own society, and in the Third and Fourth world. Our comfort, often unknown to us, is built upon the slums and shanty towns and clay huts of the deprived. It has ever been so, but it is an affront to God and our own humanity. The same writ runs in all the other drives of our nature.

There is plenty of evidence to suggest that our Western culture has capitulated to the insistent demands of the sexual drive, so that we are now awash in a complete devaluation of sex. If you have the urge, any urge, gratify it, it's bad for you not to. So the urges mount in their intensity, and the means of gratifying them become ever more complicated. Appetite is there to be gratified. Turn all these stones into bread. The tension and suffering of unfulfilled appetite is bad for you, so give in. The logic of this craving, of course, leads to personal disintegration and social chaos.

But this is not true only of individuals. We can try to turn bread into stones as a Church. We can be ashamed to address the spirit of our generation with the loving and searing word of God. We can give in to the trends of the day by simply echoing them in a desire to be popular or fashionable. This happens on all sorts of levels. We can reduce the word of God to a human word, tell people what they want to hear, give them bread when their real hunger is for God. And we end by feeding the world on stones.

The second temptation is to worship Satan for the sake of power over mankind. This is the temptation to power, the temptation that seeks control over others. It can come in many ways. In marriage, it can be the assertion of one partner's will over the other's, so that the marriage ceases to be a partnership and becomes a tyranny, however tender and disguised. The same is true of our relationships with our children. We can dominate and control them in a way that denies their own integrity and freedom. These forms of dominance are usually the result of a towering confidence in our own judgement on almost all matters. Montaigne said of the medieval practice of burning heretics: 'It is rating our conjectures highly to roast people alive for them.' Many of the things that we are so superhumanly confident about *are* conjectures, our own hunches or preferences, yet in the name of these we'll stunt and limit the freedom of others to be themselves, we'll roast them with our own certainties. This temptation has an important word to say to the Church. The world has its way of handling power. In a democratic system, the various centres of power are balanced against each other, so that none can take over completely. There is a realistic awareness that those who wield power must be watched, and that there must be instruments for controlling their misuse of power. There is a balance of forces on permanent alert. This is the model of the world, and it has invaded the Church, but it was not the way of Christ. In the Church, as in the world, we have groups playing power-games, asserting their will over others, and having it thwarted by the counter-organization of other groups. We have adopted certain aspects of the democratic model, with its pessimistic realism about the misuse of power. Christ gave us a different model, the model of service, the model of slavery. We are not to be split up into competing power groups or interest groups, all trying to get as much of their own way as possible. Our model is that of the slave who serves others, not himself. 'He that would be great among you, let him be your servant.' What a hard lesson that is to learn! We'd much rather get our own way, fight for it by our own methods, and only give in at the end. Well, the Church won't witness to Christ like that! We won't witness to Christ by horse-trading or pressurizing or insisting on our own way, but only by trying to be of service to others. We are not to model ourselves on a democracy in which the rival power groups warily counterbalance each other's power, but (if I were to make a word from the Greek for slave, *doulos*) on a *doulocracy*, in which we regard ourselves as being at the service of all the others and, above all, of Christ.

The third temptation is the most subtle and difficult of all. It is the temptation for Christ to throw himself from the pinnacle of the Temple, to test the love of God. If the first temptation is physical and the second is psychological, then this temptation is most certainly spiritual and intellectual. It is the temptation to make God conform to our standards and expectations, to remove all those aspects of the faith which embarrass our cleverness, our modern sophistication. And there is a danger here that we'll go too far in rejecting it. God has given us minds and means us to use them, so our faith must be reasonable; it must be one that we can give an account of and, at least partially, explain. But there is a difference between a reasonable faith and a faith in reason. There is a kind of person who won't or can't make the act of faith. They want everything worked out, so that faith becomes an effortless movement along a well-argued statement. They remove the paradoxes and mysteries of Christian doctrine, in order to make them more acceptable to the mind of the age. There comes a point in our dealing with God when we have to leave all that behind and simply thrust out into the dark, blindly, towards him. He challenges us, speaks a word to our hearts, and we must simply get up and go, no questions asked. We are never told in advance that it is right and safe. We are to go at that moment, when the moment comes, just as we are, without final assurance or certainty. God cannot give us the proof we demand, any more than love can prove itself to those who fear they have it not. That kind of fear and insecurity never gets enough proof. There would always have to be one more leap from the pinnacle of the temple, one more demonstration from God that he really was there. And we would remain on the bank of our own uncertainty for ever and a day. Faith does not give us that kind of assurance, that kind of certainty, and there is no point in demanding it. It has been known for centuries that the only real knowledge of God comes after the leap of faith and never before. It is only as you move more deeply into the strange darkness of faith that assurance grows.

This temptation, above all others, afflicts the preacher and the Christian teacher. There is a constant temptation to make the faith an easy and effortless exercise in thought by making the odd excision of embarrassing obscurities *here*, and then neatly stitching things up *there*. You remove all the turbulence and scandal, all the darkness and lightning, all the horror and dread, and the strange ways of God with men, and you produce a sort of synthetic article, which goes down without effort or decision, like processed cheese from which all the tang and all the smell has been purged. Much modern theology does that, so that we end up, not with the Gospel, but with that part of it which the reigning scholars happen to approve at the moment.

There is another, perhaps an opposing danger. This is the temptation, not to make Christianity reasonable and congenial to the spirit of the age, but to demand of God great showings of power, so that his reality will confront and convince the world with unavoidable majesty. How often have I read books by eager and enthusiastic Christians who claim that if we'll but do this and that, God will send down upon us a power which will overwhelm the unbelievers and have them queuing up to get into church. Well, there is a power that God gives us, as I tried to show in the last chapter, but it is frequently disconcerting in its methods. We must not tempt God by asking for the kind of power-play *we* want. It is up to God what he does with us, and he has a strange weakness for failure as the mode of his presence in the world.

The temptations of Christ in the wilderness stand as a permanent model of the ways in which we try to turn the will of God to the service of the self. They provide us with an endless topic for meditation, an endless commentary on the pathology of our selfhood which would use even the power and grace of God for its own ends, if it could lay hold of it. The Gospel tells us that Christ felt these temptations with particular acuteness: the temptation to accept the world's estimate of its own needs; the temptation to play with power 'in a good cause'; the temptation to turn the love of God into something we can manipulate for the sake of measurable success. From all these temptations and their ramifications we must be broken and emptied. The Grace of God is not a commodity with which we can deal loosely. We have been taken by God, blessed by God, now we must ask for the courage to be broken by God, all the time keeping our face towards the joy that is before us, and our mind fixed on the love that undergirds us, held up by the knowledge that angels minister to us.

13. TRANSCENDING

I have been wrestling with the attempt of the self to find God by allowing itself to be taken, blessed, broken and given away. Those of us who want to find God are desperate to find a way towards him, even if it means giving up the self. We shudder as we contemplate it, but the way of sacrifice does, at times, beckon. And it is here that we run into a wall. Does not this desire still reflect that pathology of the self which I have drawn attention to at point after point in this book? It is a paradoxical situation. We try to figure out ways to let God into our lives, because we get no satisfaction out of selfishness and because we genuinely, some of the time, want to experience the reality of God. We want our hearts to burn within us. We want to be single-minded in our devotion. We want to have that eagle faith that simply soars away. And even if we don't quite want all these things, we do, at least, want to want them! We are probably also very tired of the way we get in our own way; tired of our hesitations; tired of our inability to find some solid ground to live on; tired of our own cynicism, or of our anxieties and depressions; and tired of all our unfulfilled hungers, tired of all the things we cannot shake off, like a sleepy giant bound by a multitude of silken threads. Yes, we are tied and bound by this self we long to escape from, yet even our programmes for escape only entrench and confirm the bondage, because they are always programmes conceived by the self on behalf of the self. Isn't the self's longing to be free of itself but a refined form of selfishness? Think of some aspects of the programme I have outlined: the self must get itself into a position where God can take it and consecrate it and break it. And that programme depends for its success on the cooperation of the self and on the self's deepest longings. Paul was speaking for us all when that cry was torn from him as he contemplated the maze of his own imprisoning selfhood: 'Wretched man that I am! Who will deliver me from this body of death?'

One of the most mysterious things about man is the strange need to get away from himself. The attempt at liberation, at escape, can be represented by the figure of a cross. If you place the self at the centre of the cross, where the bars intersect, there are three directions it can take in trying to get away from itself. The most common and the easiest is what is called Downward Transcendence, transcendence simply standing for this craving to get out of the self. Downward transcendence can be harmless, but it can be dangerous and an ultimately destructive form of escape. It includes all those artificial means which buy release for a time and at a price: it obviously includes drink and drugs, but there is scarcely anything that cannot be used as a compulsive form of escape from imprisoning selfhood. Whatever it is, it represents a formidably heart-breaking and futile attempt to escape from the torment of being the self. The result is usually only an increase in desperation and self-contempt. Downward Transcendence is the major growth industry of our times. Think of the billions of pounds that go into this vast escape enterprise and all its ramifications. More tragically, think of lives stunted and deformed by their dependence upon it.

Then there is Lateral Transcendence, side-ways transcendence. This is normally thought of as high-culture, and it is reckoned to be a more wholesome and satisfying method of release than the other. It includes many of humanity's greatest artistic and musical achievements, and our enjoyment of them and ability to escape for a time into them. All are attempts, when used by the consumers of culture, to transcend or escape from the self. And they work for a time, but they can never achieve that real escape we long for, because, though higher in nature than Downward Transcendence, they are essentially human and limited in their ability to take us from ourselves. Both forms of Transcendence are essentially extensions of selfhood, extensions of human activity. They never succeed in prising the self free.

Only Upward Transcendence can do that, because only here is the other agent involved, the eagle that can sweep down upon us and take us away from ourselves and the cross upon which we are impaled. Upward Transcendence is the path to God. It is the only opening out of the trap. It is the only final way out of the maze of the self. Or is it? It is still all very selfish, is it not? It is still this little plastic slug we call the self that we are intent on finding release from, and this is where the final blow comes. Poor dear, the self has already accepted with a sigh that it must be taken and set apart and broken up, if it is to find its real direction, its escape from the maze. Now it is told that it must face the fact that none of this will achieve the desired end of escape from the prison, unless and until that desire which initiated the whole process is abandoned too! Do you see what this means? So far we have engaged ourselves on the task of completely abandoning the self to God. But there is one final chain of selfishness that binds us, and that is the very desire to be done with the self: because that desire, that motive, is still an expression, the most refined expression possible, but still an expression of selfhood that haunts and dominates us. How can we shake this off? Who *will* deliver us from this body?

By recognizing, I think, that none of this applies to us at all! It is too much for us. We must attempt it, but we know it is impossible. And the only thing that saves us from heart-break is the knowledge that it is the way of *Jesus* and that, somehow, we are able to grow into him, because he followed the way for us. It was for our sake that he sanctified himself, gave himself up. Only by abandoning himself totally to God could God use his humanity to the full in ministry to the world. And that is what happened. He was given away for the world's sake. He was taken, blessed, broken and given up, and he became, thereby, a means of grace and a vehicle of the eternal charity for the whole world. It was not his own salvation, his own peace, his own inner harmony which was achieved: it was the redemption of the whole world. And do you see the amazing difference? We waste our time if we come to pretend to love God if we are not prepared to love, and love costingly the world which is the object of his everlasting love. Yet, how can we? I do not want to alter a word of what I have written so far, yet I am convinced, in Paul's phrase, that it is 'refuse', if it is not held in the mystery of Christ. When all is said, and much has to be said, we must give up any attempt to develop a spiritual life that is not rooted and grounded in the Crucified. It is to the cross we must turn, as we turn and turn upon our own crosses, in the hope that we may be found in him.

'For his sake I have suffered the loss of all things, and count them as refuse, in order that I may gain Christ and be found in him, not having a righteousness of my own, based on law, but that which is through faith in Christ, the righteousness from God that depends on faith: that I may know him and

the power of his resurrection, and may share his sufferings, becoming like him in his death, that if possible I may attain the
resurrection from the dead.'   Phil. 3.8–11

I saw a new heaven and a new earth
Revelation 21.1

EPILOGUE

Miriam is a young mother in her early thirties. During the Sixties she was deeply involved in the drug-scene and drop-out culture. After a series of bad 'trips' she became seriously disturbed and spent the next five years in and out of mental hospital. Nothing seemed to help, and she was the despair of her family. Then she was converted to Christ. She got to know a group of young Pentecostal Christians, and through them she gave her life to Christ. Since that moment her life has been transformed. Jesus is the central fact of her life. She is a devoted wife and mother and helper of the needy. A gentle radiance surrounds her and all her actions are motivated by strong, but simple piety. Part of her charm is that, though she is now a convinced Christian and talks of her Lord with unselfconscious directness, she has never lost the offbeat style of the counter-culture. She is a member of a local congregation and through her love and ministry a number of other young, recently converted Christians have joined the fellowship. Like her, they are lovingly impatient of much that goes on in the Church. They feel certain that the Church will only win the world if it recovers a simple but total trust in the living Jesus. Their own life is evidence of that. They know that Jesus lives and that he can raise the dead to newness of life.

Hamish is in the same congregation and is the same age. He teaches at the University. He was brought up in a very strict religious family who firmly opposed all questioning of religious truth. His early years built layers of unresolved conflict into his mind and he is only now unravelling the past. He is almost obsessively sceptical and questioning. Nothing is taken on trust or authority. All must be ruthlessly questioned, because men and women have an age-old weakness for intellectual short-cuts; because they have a built-in tendency to search for emotional bromides which dull the rigours of existence. Hamish will shelter from no question; he will hide from no doubt. He is honest enough to be sceptical of his own scepticism, to doubt his own doubts, so he has never fallen for the mirror image of fundamentalist religion, which is fundamentalist atheism. He lives on a permanent knife-edge of uncertainty.

In a strange way, he is still able to cling by a single finger to the ancient liturgy of the Church. Unable to affirm privately any creed, he is yet able to achieve some identification with a worshipping community in a place where prayer has been valid, though rarely for him. His membership of the Church is rueful and ironic: he tends to watch from afar, and he has a strong fellow-feeling for Nicodemus who came to Jesus by night.

Jeff is in his mid-twenties. He's a trainee teacher who is currently 'occupying' the offices of the Principal of the College. He says he won't leave till he's carried out, and his friends believe him. He's that sort of person. He came back from two years voluntary work in South America a complete political and theological radical. The state of the world has him in a permanent rush of anger. He has seen the effects of international capitalism on the Third World. He has lived in the shanty towns of South America. He saw a rich elite growing fat on hand-outs from wealthy international companies, maintaining their position with all the hideous apparatus of the modern police-state. Now he is totally dedicated to the overthrow of the international system which holds fast so many of God's children in misery and iron. He sees the Church, with its predominantly middle-class membership, as one of the great bulwarks of this obscene state of affairs. He sees it as obsessed with its own comfort and survival. He rejects the piety of Miriam as simply a spiritual narcotic, an emotional 'high', which is condemned by its political indifferentism. Last week he accused Hamish in a bruising argument of being simply, 'another, bloody, castrated intellectual, who can't make up his mind which sock to put on first in the morning'. When he's not campaigning against the investment policies of the Ecclesiastical Commissioner, he's organizing petitions against his Church's decision to rebuild the altar and re-guild the reredos.

Barney is in his late forties, and he doesn't know what's happened to the Church he's been a member of since he was confirmed at Rugby in 1942. He's a businessman. He sends his children to expensive schools, and has been a member of the Parochial Church Council for fifteen years. He's not a hypocrite, though he sometimes wonders what his membership of the Church means. He's not the ardent type and can't stand intellectual agonizing. He never goes to any of the new-fangled house-groups that have recently sprung up in the Church, or the study-cells which always seem to be advertising 'prayer workshops' or 'praise sessions'; and he's not sure, anyway, if he'd be allowed into the seminar called: 'The Marxist interpretation of Christ's economic theories'. He tends to keep his head down during sermons nowadays. Oddly enough, though he's not given to self-analysis, and though he never talks about his religion to anyone, he's beginning to identify with the outcasts and sinners who people the pages of the Gospel, those unfortunates who were fixed in a permanent state of ritual impurity by the righteous Jews of our Lord's day. He's developing a theory of his own: for Publican and Sinner, read Capitalist. What cheers him, in a private way, is the known fact that Jesus seemed to enjoy dining with unrespectable characters. Who knows, he might even have stooped to have the odd lunch with him at the New Club!

Miriam. Hamish. Jeff. Barney. And Roderick. Roderick is the rector of the Church they all go to. It would be inaccurate to say that the cross-currents and competing pressures of his congregation had made him schizophrenic. No; they have made him multiphrenic. Not schizoid—multoid! His problem is that he warmly identifies with all four of them. But they are four and he is one. How can he agree with them all and be one person?

He loves Miriam and, like her, he too went through a Charismatic conversion experience some years ago. For awhile he was filled with a real, almost intoxicated joy in the Lord. The bible was alive! Prayer was not a duty but a source of intense happiness. He was filled with a new love for his people. But then, like Hamish, the wee man climbed back onto his shoulder and he started asking and probing and doubting. So now what is he? On his knees in a prayer-group he can still, at times, recapture that original and tearful surge of faith. But in his study he is riven by doubt and accusation of futility. And he has a soft spot for Jeff. Jeff fills him with anger and guilt and exhilaration. He see in him what he once was himself, the campaigner travelling light, naked and poor following the naked Christ. Time has brought complexity; but has it not, perhaps, also brought corruption? Has the world filled his soul, he wonders, and stolen his crown? Is he not now, an exceedingly comfortable Christian, tamed by the charms of a world he once sought to deny? Yet he loves Barney, too, and cannot disapprove of him. He respects the way he cuts off the unanswerable questions and just gets on with the job which is making him rich. He respects his complete lack of self-righteousness, the embarrassed integrity which shies away from religious talk, yet nurses a quiet love for Christ. No wonder Roderick wonders who he is—

'A man so various that he seem'd to be
Not one, but all mankind's epitome.
Stiff in opinions, always in the wrong;
Was everything by starts, and nothing long.'

Late one evening recently, Roderick went into Church to pray. As is not unusual with him, he fell asleep, and as he slept he dreamed. He heard a voice saying to him, 'This is the new Pentecost'. And then he saw the followers of Christ gathered together in one place and they began to speak in different ways as the Spirit gave them utterance. One poured forth her love of Jesus in a prayer of great beauty. Her face shone, and gradually others came out of the shadows and joined her, and the place where they were was filled with praise. When the prayer ceased, they stood there still, their arms held up to heaven in an ecstasy of adoration. Then a young man stepped forward, his face twisted in anguish and longing, and he began to speak haltingly, strangely interrogating an unseen presence, known yet unknown. As he spoke, others joined him, some with books still in their hands and questions writ upon their faces. Their voices searched the air, and they, too, were held in the circle, as their voices slowly ceased. Over there a young man started shouting, his face dark with anger and pain. He was pointing to a large company which no man could number, of the halt and the maimed, the bleared and the crazed, the ragged and the broken, who stood on the outside of the circle. The circle opened, and the strange motley entered and gathered round the young man till he ceased his crying. Then in the silence, on the outer edge of the circle, someone tried to suppress a sob with that painful catching of the breath that tears the chest. Quietly the circle opened to reveal a well-dressed man, his face contorted with grief and confusion, tears pouring down his face. Many there were that joined him, upright men, in pin-striped suits, clutching briefcases, tentative now, unsure of themselves, yet held in the circle. Nothing, it seemed, could be kept out of that radiant circle. It extended to the horizon, a great multitude which no man could number, from every nation, from all tribes and people and tongues, each praising the Lamb of God according to the manner of the knowledge given unto him. And soon the grass and the stones and the birds in flight were crying out to that centre where stood the lamb slain from the foundation of the world. And then he saw that all creation revolved round that strange centre, each thing was held in that mysterious orbit no matter how furiously it plunged away into space. Finally, he saw the whole Universe, every immeasurable fraction of it; all of time, and the vast reaches of the ages; and he saw all struggle and loss, every wound and battle tumult; all separation and going down into dust was there; and he saw every leaf that ever was, and all love and the singing of it; beauty there was, and failure, and every road not taken; each heart-stopping moment since the foundation of the earth, held together at last in one colossal shout of praise, the great and final Amen of a transfigured creation: 'Amen. Blessing and glory and wisdom and thanksgiving and honour and power and might be to our God for ever and ever. Amen.'

Roderick woke with that exultant shout ringing in his ears. And he remembered those mysterious words of St Augustine: 'God is a circle, whose centre is everywhere and whose circumference is nowhere.' And there in the dark church he laughed, laughed at his fears and the smallness of men and women that they must limit and define, not only each other, but the very ways of God. 'Amen!' he shouted, as he remembered the illimitable love of God, that long rope that stretches right into hell itself and out the other side. 'Amen!' he chortled, as he made his way home past the startled promenaders. 'Amen, to each and to it all. for the Lord God Omnipotent reigneth!' 'Amen', he whispered, as the tears started to flow, 'Amen.'